Melbourne College of Divinity
Bicentennial Lectures

IAN BREWARD

Australia

"The Most Godless Place Under Heaven"?

With good wishes to Professor Denzler
Ian Breward.

Lutheran Publishing House

First printed by Beacon Hill Books, 1988.
Second printing, Lutheran Publishing House, July 1991

Acknowledgment is made to the
Melbourne College of Divinity
for the grant they provided
which assisted the publication
of this book.

ISBN 0 9594192 3 3

Cover design: Trudy Hill
Printed and published by
Lutheran Publishing House
205 Halifax Street, Adelaide, South Australia 0752-91

Contents

Foreword

Recent books on Australia's cultural heritage have given serious attention to the place of religion and of religious institutions in our life. There have also been some monographs of a scholarly kind such as that of Arnold Hunt on the history of Methodism in South Australia, and of course, the massive and most important work of Patrick O'Farrell on Australian Roman Catholic history and his many insights into the place of religion in Australian life; but we have lacked what Professor Ian Breward now offers in these lectures, a review of the history of the Christian Churches in Australia from 1788 until the present day which alludes to the problems which they had to face, and analyses with both honesty and sensitivity the presuppositions with which they faced them. We needed a professional historian to do this; and perhaps it helped to have a New Zealand historian, become Australian, to enable us to see that history with a degree of detachment.

Of the many things which these lectures may help us to understand better about ourselves, two may be mentioned—although they are in somewhat paradoxical relation one to the other. The first is that from the beginning the Churches have all had some formidable personalities in their leadership: and Church Assemblies, Synods, Conferences have never been backward in declaring their minds on public issues. Ecclesiastical circles have not been territory in which to look for the shrinking violet. Even today the press, and perhaps the public, tends to show more interest in what bishops and moderators and synods say than in what the majority, or even a minority, of lay members of the Churches do about social questions.

The second element in our history to which Professor Breward alludes again and again is the contribution made by Church members often anonymously, not seeking the praise of men, to civic life. This ranges from generous benefaction to the founding of 'libraries, savings banks, temperance and benevolent societies, Mechanics Institutes... The power of creative minorities and individuals is very clear in the early history of the Australian churches' (p. 9). It is still true that what Christians have to offer Australia through their professions, through initiatives taken in social welfare, through care for those at a disadvantage, is much more important than what ecclesiastical authority has to say about these things.

It might cast light on all this if we were to reflect a little more on the insight of Professor Breward that all the British Churches in Australia had to become 'gathered churches by winning lay support, coaxing money out of members and adherents who knew nothing about regular giving to churches which had been hitherto supported by tithes, the wealthy and endowments'. With this went a democratising of Church life. It would be interesting to trace further the influence of this on social democratic institutions in Australia, local government, trade unions, professional associations, our many houses of parliament. The story has been told elsewhere of the influence of the Church meeting of Congregationalism on the development of democratic institutions in England and New England. Did the Churches in Australia prepare the way for the greater degree of participation in the making of decisions affecting their lives now claimed by many groups in society? Or have Churchmen and women forgotten to make the translation?

These and a host of other questions are raised by Professor Breward's lucid and rather modest lectures. It is to be hoped that under his guidance a number of younger Church historians will further investigate the matter; and, of course, we look forward to more from Professor Breward's pen. He cannot stop now.

Davis McCaughey
Government House
Melbourne

Preface

This book is a revised version of the Bicentennial Lectures sponsored by the Melbourne College of Divinity. A survey necessarily omits much significant detail, but I have attempted an overview for people who want an indication of the main themes of Australian church history. Eventually, this work will be complemented by a much more detailed study and a collection of documents.

I am indebted to the manuscript librarians in the National Library and State Libraries for access to and help in using their collections. The archivists of the Victorian Synod and the Northern Synod of the Uniting Church have been very helpful. The staff of the Mollison Library, Trinity College, the Joint Theological Library, Ormond College and Moore College have also been indispensable in directing me to material I could easily have overlooked. Perceptive comments and criticisms have been given by Drs A. Cooper, K. Manley, L. McIntosh and M. Porter. My wife has given her usual support and encouragement. The Theological Hall secretaries have put my typescript into order with their usual patience and helpfulness.

I wish to thank the following for permission to use quotations: Cambridge University Press, which has reprinted Professor O'Farrell's 1982 essay "The cultural ambivalence of Australian religion" in S. L. Goldberg and F. B. Smith, *Australian Cultural History*, Melbourne 1988; Archbishop Keith Rayner of Adelaide; the Legion of Mary and the Australian Catholic Truth Society for extracts from Father J. A. Connellan.

Ian Breward

CHAPTER ONE:

From Prison to Colony 1788–1836

The words of James Denney in the lectures' title reflect a Scottish Presbyterian theologian's view of the difficulties many migrants had in recognising true religion in their adopted land. Reports of lax religious observance in the bush and the depravity of convicts could give an impression of much more godless communities than existed in Britain. In fact there was plenty of British godlessness. There it was socially and legally masked by the social prestige and power of the churches, especially those which were established. Their failure to minister adequately to the whole community can be seen not only in the convicts' behaviour, but also in the irreligion of the soldiers guarding them and in many of the free settlers.

This failure was unmistakably visible in New South Wales, where many of the traditional supports of religious observance were absent.[1] To create the institutions and networks of the Christian community from nothing amongst the heathen had a certain romance. Performing a similar mission among convicts confronted the chaplains with challenges, which the British churches largely ignored. The leaders of the British churches took no interest in the spiritual welfare of the convicts. It was some time before they could be persuaded that they had some responsibility for the free settlers. It was government and lay action which provided the beginnings of Christian presence, in what was initially an extensive gaol. There were few models for the redemption of the convicted criminal, apart from initiatives by Quakers like Elizabeth Fry and some preaching by Evangelicals.

The fragility of religious authority among the underclasses of British society can be seen in the accounts of voyages out on the convict ships. These voyages were often a shattering introduction for chaplains, who discovered how dependent they were on outside authority even to provide enough order to be heard. Their hearers were often too brutalised to hear what seemed the language of moral superiority and middle class arrogance. Gaolers and chaplains alike regarded their charges, at some times, as sub-human and beyond any persuasion but violent repression.[2]

There were several patterns of pastoral response to this frontier of need—provision of services, care for the sick and dying, the building of churches and schools, personal dealing and magisterial sentence of the obdurate and rebellious. Richard Johnson, the first chaplain, was appointed through the good offices of influential Evangelicals, but a Roman Catholic offer to send two priests with the first fleet was refused by the authorities.[3] They instructed Phillip to ensure that the Book of Common Prayer was read each Sunday and Holy Day. His oath of allegiance at the foundation of the colony included a rejection of the doctrine of transubstantiation, presumably to ensure that no taint of Romanism entered even a prison colony.

First Chaplains

Johnson was a firm Evangelical, but he had a genuine compassion for his flock and gave himself without stint to impossible pastoral demands. The strain of up to sixty funerals a month would tax the resources of the hardiest chaplain, even if he had the support of the authorities. Add to that the absence of the facilities that British clergy took for granted, the strain of travel in all weathers, the struggle of making a glebe yield something towards the support of a family and a constant struggle with military authorities who were at times downright hostile and obstructive, and one can begin to understand that he returned to England with a sense of failure. Until he erected a simple building at his own expense in 1793, he either had to take services in the open or in a variety of makeshift buildings. He had a dreadful struggle to extract a refund from the authorities and when the building was burnt by an arsonist, it was not replaced for some time.

Nor was Johnson when he returned home in 1800. His colleague Samuel Marsden, who had arrived in 1794, worked alone for seven years ministering to over six thousand.[4] Gifted with an iron constitution, deep Evangelical convictions and a fair share of Yorkshire obstinacy, he felt desperately isolated and frustrated at times, when he contrasted the pastoral needs of the colony with the limits of his own physical capacity. Though he coped better than Johnson with the touchy and often tyrannical governors and their officials, he was at times very badly treated. He waited twenty years for his glebe and was denied the freedom to introduce even modest innovations in worship to make services more attractive. Macquarie's behaviour displayed the petulance and pettiness of a frustrated martinet, but Marsden too was difficult and acquired the reputation of a very turbulent priest among Colonial Office administrators.

Marsden's Evangelicalism enabled him to lay the foundations of inter-denominational co-operation with Congregationalists and Wesleyans. When a group of London Missionary Society workers arrived for refuge in Sydney in 1798, after escaping from Tahiti, Marsden was very generous with help and made use of their skills in teaching and preaching in the Parramatta area and elsewhere. Similarly he gave help to Samuel Leigh, the first Wesleyan missionary who arrived without official permission in 1815. Relations between them were later to cool, but initially Marsden was happy to have yet another to help with the ever-growing tasks of pastoral care. He also acted as agent for the London Missionary Society, as well as founding a mission to the Maori in New Zealand, in 1814. Indeed, the sheer range of Marsden's activities was quite daunting and it was hardly surprising that at times he made bad decisions and was insensitive to others. By 1803 he had built a substantial church in Parramatta and was a constant recruiter of clergy like William Cowper and Robert Cartwright, who made a notable contribution to the development and extension of the Church of England. Marsden's future son-in-law, Thomas Hassall founded the first Sunday School in December 1815 and then became the first Australian ordinand, returning from England as a minister in 1822.

Marsden was also an extraordinarily successful farmer from the time that he received his first land grant and assigned servants in 1794 to his death in 1838 when his estates of 4745 hectares were valued for probate at thirty thousand pounds. He was one of the founders of the colony's wool industry and its superior Merino flocks. Even if his social origins were ordinary, he left his family securely in the upper class. His very success limited his ability to minister without the complication of social distance and wealth. Appointment as a magistrate in 1795 was a common clergyman's role in England, but it introduced elements into Marsden's ministry which have provided later generations with material for dismissive comments about the flogging parson, which overshadow his real achievements.

Some of his sentences were severe and aroused hostile comment at the time. His brutal attempts to elicit information about possible Irish convict revolt have to be seen against the background of official reaction to the Castle Hill Rising of 1804 and the deep feelings that Marsden shared about the Irish potential for villainy.[5] At this point he was very much a child of his Protestant culture. Marsden nonetheless optimistically believed, like many other Protestants, that if Catholics were left to Protestant influences, the rising generation would forsake and forget their traditional faith.

Nor was Marsden able to break out of his convictions about the stain of criminality to allow himself to extend the hand of friendship to emancipists, or to work with them in public life. Equality before a forgiving God remained for the next life. Given the numbers of convicts, emancipists and their children in New South Wales—90% of the population in 1819—it was hardly surprising that free settlers sought to protect their religious and moral purity. Determined that their definition of culture, religion and morality should triumph, many of Australia's early Christians laid a heavy emphasis on the importance of moral respectability, as a testimony to a redeemed life. The finer graces of intellectual and spiritual refinement had to take second place to morality because of the struggle to survive and to repress the violence, dishonesty, drunkenness, immorality and mockery of religion which threatened the delicate plants of civilisation.

It was not surprising that convicts and emancipists should reject the compulsory religion and morality of the Protestant ruling class. Away from churches and parsons in the bush, religious observance was not a priority at all. Farmworkers, bullockies and sawyers were often indifferent to religion or cynical about the motives of travelling parsons who occasionally crossed their paths, though the remarkable Quaker travellers, Backhouse and Walker had many warm and hospitable encounters with bush dwellers. Having to deal with such attitudes without the advantages of class superiority and legal authority placed Australian clergy under severe pressure and speedily removed some of the less pleasant features of establishment mentality, and dogmatic assertiveness. Communication meant meeting the hostile, apathetic and deprived on their own terms, even if there was yet little recognition that this clientele was largely a product of the British churches' inability to minister to the urban poor and underclasses. There were few settlers in the early years of New South Wales like the Scots settlers on the Hawkesbury who built their 'Ebenezer' at Portland Head in 1809 and worshipped regularly under the catechist John Mein until they received the reluctant services of the Rev. John McGarvie in 1826.

The beginnings of convict settlement in Van Diemen's Land were similar, except that the Chaplain, Rev. Robert Knopwood, was indisputably a gentleman, did not clash with the authorities and exercised a faithful ministry without 'enthusiasm', like many of his English counterparts.[6] At the first service there, on 26 February, 1804 Knopwood preached on Psalm107:43 and underlined Divine beneficence. His journals reveal a deep piety and an unobtrusive kindness. Creating the basic buildings and roads, and hacking farms out of the bush, was the dominant theme of the early years. When Arthur arrived there in 1824 he made a serious attempt to reform his convicts according to Evangelical ideas. There were also serious problems with the Aborigines who made the expansion of settlement very difficult by their skilful attacks. Arthur's costly attempt to flush them out was a failure, but the appointment of the Wesleyan G.A. Robinson as Protector and the banishment of a small group of defeated and dispirited survivors to remote islands led to the eventual extinction of those who had not intermarried and cohabited with whites.

Race Relations

In New South Wales it had been the same story. The official good intentions of the authorities towards Aborigines were vitiated by mutual incomprehension, rivalry for land and water and brutal exploitation of women. The attempt of Macquarie to found a school in 1814 was a failure which closed in 1826. There were no responses to the missionary concern of Marsden and others. The almost uniform reaction of observers of Aboriginal customs was one of disgust and contempt for such apparently wretched specimens of humanity—if they were human at all. Any prospects of civilising such a people seemed remote, though some observers like the Rev. James Gunther recognised their intelligence and capacity to learn English and reading. Dr. J. D. Lang in 1834 noted in his evidence to the Select Committee on Aborigines that they had nothing which could be styled worship, though they did have a belief in superior beings both good and evil. That negative judgement on aboriginal religion is still alive and well. In 1985, Mr. J. Bjelke-Petersen (the then Premier of Queensland) commented in similar terms on Aboriginal beliefs: "I do not believe in that sort of religion, because, to my mind, it is not a religion. Members of the National Party believe in the Christian faith as it is set out clearly and distinctly in the Bible."[7]

By 1825, there had been many episodes of punitive action against aboriginal raiders. Marsden suggested that missionaries living in the interior among the tribes might solve the problems of order. No volunteers were forthcoming and muskets were generally regarded by settlers as better pacifiers than missions. The failure of the Wesleyan Mission begun by the Rev. William Walker in 1821 was well known. Nor was the experienced Congregational missionary, L.E. Threkeld any more successful near Lake Macquarie. The London Missionary Society found his expenses too heavy to continue and though he remained there for seventeen years 1825–41, doing pioneer translation work, the people either died off or moved away. The Church Missionary Society's work at Wellington Valley, begun in 1832, also ended in failure despite initial optimism. The Aborigines were not specially interested in literacy and resisted attempts to turn them into small Sabbath-keeping farmers or artisans. They were quite capable of putting difficult religious questions to their would-be mentors and pointed out inconsistencies in white morality. The efforts of the missionaries were undermined by hostile settlers and they were often more attractive sources of trade goods and food than missionaries. Despite both Broughton's and

Polding's efforts and genuinely humanitarian convictions, they did not succeed in persuading many of their flock to accept their views. The colonial newspapers were hostile to the blacks and frequently reflected the view that the Aborigines were destined to disappear.

The troubled relationship of white British and European settlers to the estimated half million Aborigines whose tribes had inhabited this continent for over forty thousand years often exposed the raw edges of human passion and evil. The churches were largely helpless to deal with racism and oppression when economic interests and survival were involved. Recent study has underlined the complexity and richness of Aboriginal religions and the adaptability of tribal societies, not to mention the inseparability of religion and everyday life.[8] It is not too difficult to see some of the cultural blindness of our forebears about Aboriginal culture. Even the sensitive Quaker, James Backhouse, contrasted the folly of corroborees and their unrestrained dancing, with the sobriety and order of Protestant religion, which banished dancing for the sake of the discipline of holiness. Detecting our own cultural and religious blindspots is much harder. Just as Solzhenitsyn argues that there can be no healing of his homeland until its people come to terms with the evil which led to the death of millions in the name of ideology, Australians have yet to come to terms with the spiritual and moral implications of the conquest of this continent, with the murder, violence and degradation which is interwoven with the wealth and achievement of some of our most important industries and families. Paradoxically those evils co-exist with a long tradition of service and compassion which has many Christian roots, even if it has not been immune from exploitation by the politically and economically powerful.

There are religious roots to this communal heartlessness and racism, for the history of the Aborigines' ill-treatment has some parallels with the ways in which religion has been a partner in the English marginalisation of other social and cultural groups. The churches have had many leaders with the conviction that English is the language of civilisation and progress. The Cornish language has vanished; Gaelic and Welsh barely survive. The mini-languages of the Aborigines were difficult to learn and the cost of publishing in the languages of such small communities was daunting, even if enough translators could be found. English seemed to be the key to conversion and civilisation. There is a long tradition among Christians that conversion means accepting the evangelist's culture and religion. The converts' past was replaced by the tradition of the converting community. Evangelical Protestants underlined that even more forcibly, for movement from sin to righteousness meant repudiation of the past culture, because the past culture was seen as evil.[9]

Such convictions were very susceptible to cultural manipulation and none of the early missionaries appear to have seen anything in Aboriginal cultures worth preserving. In addition, there was a well developed hierarchy of religious values and attitudes to authority, which intersected with the conventions of political power in a pre-democratic British society. Lower orders were expected to keep their place and it was not for nothing that the notable Methodist, Jabez Bunting, was reputed to have proudly claimed that Wesleyans hated democracy as much as they hated sin. The manner in which the new realities opened up by conversion could be defined in middle class male terms is most clearly seen in the various strands of Methodism and Dissent. That could press heavily on women, not to mention the working class. Convicts and emancipists who wished to leave their past, were offered a new identity and a total community in which to grow a new personhood, if they opted for Evangelical conversion.

These religious patterns were even more culturally destructive of much that held Aboriginal communities together, for individual choice which rejected kin and land made one a non-person, and undermined the complex relations of religion and community law safeguarded by the elders. As for the mythology which sustained Aboriginal spirituality, that was dismissed with contempt by almost all Christian observers. They were part of a movement which among Roman Catholics and Protestants alike led away from the patterns of folk religion into a historically and doctrinally constructed religion.[10] The new land was empty of religious associations created by historic buildings and the sacred places of British folk religion. The good and evil spirits of the British Isles did not migrate to populate the mysterious bush and heat-hazed distances of the vast grasslands, let alone the threatening spaces of the yet unknown deserts.

Challenge to Establishment

It is equally important to note the inwardness of much Protestant religion, especially the varieties brought to the first colonies by Wesleyans and Dissenters. The latter, in particular, contributed much to the development of the Evangelical tradition which has been such an important part of the Protestant ethos in Australia for two centuries. Dissenters still had substantial legal disabilities in England, which lasted for much of the 19th century. One part of their reaction was to turn inward and focus their Christianity on the personal drama of salvation. That is immortalised in the writings of John Bunyan, who rejected the possibility of changing Vanity Fair. Instead one walked in this world as a stranger and pilgrim, for it was the world of the spirit that was real and shaped the external world into a theatre for holiness. Many migrants from this subculture had no political aspirations or experience. Their participation in the increasingly democratic Australian community was expressed in the proclamation of spiritual and moral absolutes. There was neither interest in or experience of the patterns of the political decision-making of this early period. Conversion was what mattered.

They were also skilled at surviving discrimination and creating a strong network around their chapel, nurturing individuals who rejected the values of the majority culture and were capable of enduring scorn and even ostracism for righteousness' sake. The Rev. F. Miller came to such a congregation founded in Hobart during 1824 and constituted a Congregational Church there in March 1832. Many Dissenters devoted their energies to a trade or business, as well as helping to found civic and community institutions which would help others, like libraries, savings banks, temperance and benevolent societies, Mechanics Institutes. Henry Hopkins, a typical Congregationalist, was active in Miller's congregation, successful in business and generous in help to others.[11] Such Christians' role in local history is one of the most important ways of tracing the influence of the churches in Australia, for such Christian citizenship did much to transform communities where the convict stain was dyed deep. The power of creative minorities and individuals is very clear in the early history of the Australian churches.

Indeed, one of the most interesting features of the first fifty difficult years of settlement is not only the replication of historic religious rivalries from Britain, though they were real, but the emergence of co-operation which would have been unusual, even unimaginable, in the mother country. It is hard for us to recreate the depth of the gulf between church and chapel, or the lack of familiarity that the English had with Irish and Scots, and *vice versa.* Members of the United Church of England and Ireland found it very difficult to cope with Dr. J.D. Lang, the first Presbyterian minister in Sydney.[12] They were not accustomed to recognise the legal equality of the Church of Scotland, even though it was written into the Act of Union between England and Scotland, passed in 1707.

From the time that he joined his brother in 1823, Lang identified with Australia. He had a strong political radicalism, impatient with inherited privilege. He had a deadly pen and great ability for discovering history and precedent that suited his own purposes. He never hesitated to defend a principle, no matter what enemies it made and he certainly never forgot a slight or insult. Initially he hoped to establish a Presbyterian cause which would include both members of the Church of Scotland and its rivals. Though he had the initial support of the Commissary-General, William Wemyss, a Secessionist, he discovered that such support meant the enmity of influential members of Governor Brisbane's administration, like Major F. Goulburn. Though Brisbane had helped the building fund for Lang's church, he did not think it appropriate to permit government aid when that was requested in 1823. The patronising reply which was published in the Sydney *Gazette* led to a barbed reply by 'Ignotus' (a Lang pseudonym) in the number published on 16 October, 1823, reminding the Governor that in terms of law the Church of Scotland did not have to accept the crumbs of Episcopal toleration, but was a fully established church, entitled to the same standing and government aid as the Episcopalians.

Once the foundation stone of Scots Church was safely laid on 1 July, 1824, Lang returned to Britain to lobby. Not only was Lang completely upheld, he was granted a stipend of three hundred pounds and one-third of the cost of the church. He also put obstructive officialdom in its place over his right to marry without the permission of the Church of England, by pointing out an Indian precedent for his position. He was initially willing to cooperate with the Anglicans in education, for he regarded this as enormously important for the future of the nation he foresaw, but he did not agree with the privilege enshrined in the Church and Schools Corporation of 1825 and became one of its most determined opponents, until it was suspended in 1829 and finally abolished in 1833.

That was one of the most important decisions for the future of the churches in Australia, for it ended exclusive Anglican establishment. A similar scheme in Canada also ended because it was clearly inappropriate politically. Lang's vision of a free Australia, which was a centre for evangelical civilisation of the Pacific region, did not persuade all his contemporaries, but it was a fascinating alternative to the pretensions of the pastoralists. It presupposed an huge influx of skilled and industrious settlers who would submerge convict and emancipist influence by their industry, education, piety and enterprise, while at the same time relieving the over-crowded cities of Scotland of their unemployed and underemployed.

Lang wrote voluminously on the subject of migration and also put large sums of his own and his family's money into high-risk ventures. Administration was his weak point and he was too busy to distinguish public, private and church funds with adequate clarity to satisfy either auditors or public. Yet with Caroline Chisholm, he did more than any others to transform the colony by bringing in clergy, teachers, skilled tradesmen and farmers, underlining how religious vision and political acumen could change the attitudes of local and London authorities. Though Lang distrusted Mrs Chisholm as a Papist wanting to subvert the Protestant character of the colony by Irish migrants, they both spent freely of their time and resources to expose abuses, to protect the needy and offer thousands the opportunity of a new life. Her achievement was the more remarkable, because she departed from the domestic role into such a public and political sphere, supported by a husband who was content to allow his wife amazing freedom.[13]

It was a tragedy for the colony that Lang and Archdeacons Scott and Broughton could not agree on the best pattern of education for the colony's children. That was due both to personal antipathy and very different understandings of education and the role of the church in the colony. Archdeacon Scott whose coming in 1825 marked the end of government control of the Church of England, gave it clearer ecclesiastical status. Scott obtained more chaplains, developed schools and regularised administration, but his personal limitations and the inability to appreciate the religious integrity of the Evangelical tradition left him at odds with some clergy. He did not manage to stay clear of the political feuds of the colony. By contrast, W.G. Broughton who replaced Scott in 1829, was an experienced churchman, with a clearly articulated vision of the role of the Church of England and its relation to State and society.[14]

His views were conservative and he was a doughty opponent of liberalism, which was becoming increasingly influential in the colony, for he saw the Church of England as the essential source of spiritual wisdom, moral insight and education in a society which was impoverished in all three. The Church was not just a useful adjunct to Government policy. It was the conscience of the community and the source of divine grace, without which the colony's search for direction would be futile. Convicts, emancipists and their children were still a substantial majority in New South Wales and even more so in Van Diemen's Land. Parish schools still only touched a minority of the eligible children, but important beginnings had been made in increasing literacy. There was however no secondary education worth speaking of and both Broughton and Lang were anxious to remedy this defect.

Though Broughton had partial success in founding the King's Schools, Lang's ambitious Australian College which had begun in 1832, was a serious rival to the King's School in Sydney. Lang believed that it was possible to provide religious education based on the Bible, acceptable to all Protestants, for that was his Scottish experience. Broughton was insistent that there was no general Christianity and that the Church of England would betray its religious trust if it consented to anything less than a Church-based system of education. He was very aware of the rivals to this hegemony in England and did not want to see them emerge in New South Wales. There was another person with strong views on the subject and that was Governor Bourke. His Irish experience persuaded him that the only satisfactory system for the colony was one which bridged the gap between Protestants and Roman Catholics by a system akin to the Irish National system, which filled in the gaps left by the church schools.

Many in the Catholic community were happy to accept Bourke's proposals, for it gave them far more than they had. That irked many Protestants who suspected a popish plot, even if they were hostile to what seemed intolerance on Broughton's part. He was adamantly opposed to a reform likely to undermine the place and responsibilities of the Church of England. He departed, like Lang, to England to lobby and after very complex negotiations, Glenelg accepted a modified version of Bourke's proposals, which included the creation of a diocese of Australia, excised from Calcutta, and the consecration of Broughton as the first Bishop of Australia at Lambeth on 14 February, 1836. Broughton had made it very plain that he could not in conscience accept consecration if he did not have freedom of action in relation to Bourke's proposal to give aid to Anglicans, Catholics and Presbyterians. He returned to the Legislative Council in time to help defeat Bourke's proposals for government schools, which would transcend denominational identity and provide the basis for a nation. That theme was to be a recurrent dream, but the strength of denominational loyalties has meant the dream has never been realised on liberal terms.

Roman Catholics

One of the major reasons for that failure has been the importance of the Roman Catholic Church in Australia. From the beginning of the colony, the number of Irish Catholics was far higher than in the British population generally. Political and social conditions in Ireland ensured that the proportion increased. Catholic Emancipation in 1829 gave Catholics in the convict colonies an opportunity to play their part in shaping a new nation, in ways that were not so open in their homeland. It is important to realise how the United States and British colonies provided an outlet for Irish aspirations and energies denied at home. Here significant religious concessions had been already made by the authorities, not from any conviction about the importance of toleration, but for the very pragmatic reason that it was believed that the presence of priests might lessen Irish convict turbulence.

Father Dixon, almost certainly unjustly convicted for his alleged role in the rising of 1798, conducted the first official Mass in May, 1803. The rising of 1804 led to the withdrawal of that concession until 1820, because of official fears of Mass providing a venue for Irish political discontent and plotting. About one fifth of the Irish prisoners could be classed as 'politicals'. The rest were criminals of varying degrees of hardihood. Though many had kept only minimal religious practice and reflected the depressed state of their church in Ireland, they were united in their detestation of compulsory attendance at Protestant services, the baptism of their children by Protestant chaplains and the absence of Catholic last rites at death. Some spoke only Gaelic and were unlikely to be blessed by the preaching of English sermons. The authorities had little understanding of Irish identity. They assumed that the nexus between nationality and religion would be speedily broken by exposure to the superior truths of Protestant religion, which would end the impact of generations of subservience to priests, and the credulity and ignorance fostered by such relationship.

Without romanticising Irish religion, the historian cannot but note their Catholicism not only survived without priestly leadership, but that there was a group of laity able to provide the foundations on which priests could later build. The arrival of the freelance Father O'Flynn in 1817 bred an official reaction much more hostile than that displayed to self-invited Methodists and Dissenters. His deportation in 1818 confirmed for some Catholics that Protestant bigotry and vindictiveness still flourished in the government. A new era began in 1820 when the British authorities approved the sending of two Catholic chaplains, Fathers J. Therry and P. Conolly. Both had serious temperamental weaknesses and they faced the same problems as their Protestant equivalents with a system which subordinated religion to other priorities. Their ecclesiastical authorities gave them little help and guidance, for like their Protestant counterparts, they had many more important priorities than convict chaplaincy or pastoral care of settlers in such a remote colony.

What is remarkable about these difficult beginnings is they still led to a degree of Catholic–Protestant co-operation which would have been unusual and perhaps impossible in Britain. Protestant subscriptions for a Catholic chapel were invited and several Protestants acted as agents for the reception of donations, while Mr. J.T. Campbell acted as Treasurer of the Fund.[15] Further appeals in 1825 and 1834 also included requests to Protestants. In part that was an expression of the poverty of the Catholic community, but it was an interesting example of a theme which occurs again and again in the history of Christianity in Australia—the ecumenism of need. The Catholic chaplains faced even heavier burdens than Protestants. Travel was exhausting and when Conolly left for Hobart, Therry was left as the only priest for a community grown to 16,000 Catholics. It was not surprising that he was often desperately tired and embroiled in disputes with his own people and the authorities. He refused to accept Macquarie's instructions not to officiate at marriages where one of the parties was a Protestant. He refused to keep out of government orphanages and leave Irish children to Protestant clergy. He refused to accept the boundaries Protestants laid down, for his priorities were very different from theirs.

At many points his ministry has interesting parallels with Lang's. He was not good at keeping accounts, he had an acid pen and tongue which frequently brought conflict. His dismissal in 1825 came over a printer's error which transformed his 'unqualified' respect for Protestant clergy into one that was 'qualified'. He was willing to resist obstructive colonial officials like the hospital superintendent who did his best to prevent Therry from administering extreme unction to the Catholic dying. He was to have very ambivalent relationships with constituted ecclesiastical authority, and the Catholic community was deeply divided about him. Nevertheless, he did much to lay the foundations for Catholic participation in public life which were consolidated by Ullathorne and Polding.

When Ullathorne arrived as Vicar-General in 1833, he did something to sort out the personal conflicts which are such a feature of migrant churches before patterns of government are regularised and lay initiatives are tamed. He was horrified at colonial depravity and the religious laxity of the Catholic community, but it was not until the arrival of Bishop J.B. Polding in September 1835 that Catholics had the episcopal leadership which could regularise anomalies and develop the normal structures of diocesan and parish life.[16] The missionary task Polding faced was enormous, with only eight priests for over 20 000 people to care for in New South Wales and over 2000 in Van Diemens Land. Broughton protested strongly, but unsuccessfully, at Polding's assumption of episcopal title and dignities. He was the first officially recognised English Catholic bishop since the Reformation, some time before the Roman Catholic hierarchy was restored in England and Scotland. Polding, like his Protestant counterparts was ill-prepared for a missionary task for which there were no precedents and never enough resources, either in clergy and religious, or in money for churches, schools and houses. Nonetheless, his achievements were notable.

Patterns of Ministry

Australian clergy certainly had to cope with a more godless society than their peers at home, with far more slender support and resources. However, significant beginnings had been made by the 1830s. Even if some of the clergy who came to Australia were misfits unable to find satisfactory employment in Britain, others provided important leadership in the colonies, especially when the proportion of free settlers began to rise dramatically and the convict system slowly lost its dominance. Building churches and chapels was a huge enough task, physically and financially. By the end of this first period Francis Greenway had created some churches of real distinction, such as St. Matthew's, Windsor. Even if other buildings for worship were much more utilitarian, churches were often the first public buildings to be erected in the bush, when squatters and settlers pushed out beyond the urban and county boundaries. Religion may not have been so important as in Britain, nor as in the United States, but its public profile was very significant in the first half century.

Given the patterns of British religious life, the building of churches and the provision of clergy was essential if a prison was to become a colony. Creation of indigenous and self-supporting churches was to be a longer task. Conversion, revival of the lapsed, education, pastoral care, rebuke of evil and apathy were all needed. Memories of national churches were all very well. All the British churches here found that they had to learn the techniques of the gathered churches by winning lay support, coaxing money out of members and adherents who knew nothing about regular giving to churches which had been hitherto supported by tithes, the wealthy and endowments. Catholics had a significant advantage in being able to call on religious orders like the Sisters of Mercy, who were committed to poverty. Protestants, however, found it a heavy burden to house and support married ministers, and to pay their passage as well. Few of the parent churches gave more than a part of these expenses, though the importance of the great Anglican societies, the Society for the Propagation of the Gospel and the Society for the Propagation of Christian Knowledge, has often been overlooked by modern historians.

The Australian churches were only partly influenced by the burgeoning missionary movement from Britain, but the Evangelical tradition which was its substantial impetus was certainly present in all the Australian Protestant churches by 1836, though it was not the only tradition in the Church of England. A more broad church pattern was discernible in the small and isolated colony of West Australia, where settlement had begun in Albany in 1826.[17] When sovereignty over all of Australia outside New South Wales was proclaimed near Perth by Captain Fremantle on 2 May, 1829 initial hopes of speedy prosperity were dashed by the poor soil and arid climate. Many colonists left, leaving only the determined and a small garrison at Swan River. This colony had two marked differences from New South Wales. It had no convicts and its settlers included a core with gentry connections and a band of Methodist colonists from Yorkshire who arrived on the"Tranby" on 3 February, 1830, planning to farm. They brought lay preachers with them to ensure that they had the means of grace from the start. They celebrated their safe landing by a beach service. Services were ecumenical from the beginning, for the Wesleyans were happy to attend Prayer Book services as well as their own meetings, at which one English visitor found the singing too loud. By 1834, they had their own simple church. In 1836 a controversial missionary to the local Aborigines arrived—the Rev. Dr. L. Giustiani who was a former Roman Catholic. He worked from July, 1836 to February, 1838 and speedily became unpopular with settlers and administration alike, for his advocacy of Aboriginal rights. The Wesleyans wrote to their British Conference in July, 1836, pleading for a missionary with facility in learning aboriginal languages, as well as having deep piety.

Such zeal and the strongly lay quality of Methodism can also be seen in Hobart where the first class meeting was held in October, 1820 led by Benjamin Nokes and George Waddy, after a missionary visit by Benjamin Carvosso earlier in 1820.[18] A chapel was rented in early 1821 and one of the earliest Sunday Schools in Australasia began in May, 1821. By 1833, there had been such development that church membership was greater than on the mainland. Their first District Meeting was held in 1836, under the Rev. Joseph Orton. Methodists in Hobart began the first public library in Australia on 19th September, 1825. Some remarkable laymen were nurtured in this Wesleyan community, including Henry Reed and Walter Powell, both of whom were to become substantial benefactors. Reed arrived in 1826, virtually penniless, and finally found religious peace and prosperity in Launceston.[19] He was a local preacher and Sunday School Superintendent, with a passion for evangelism, which was ultimately to lead him to give important support to William Booth, founder of the Salvation Army. Reed was also interested in the possibilities of Port Phillip Bay where Batman had purchased land in 1835. He was one of the first to preach there, though other laymen like Dr. Thomson and J.P. Fawkner organised simple community services from the earliest stages of settlement. Orton was the first minister to conduct worship there on 24 April, 1836, returning at a later stage to give Wesleyans invaluable leadership from 1840 to 1842.

By 1836, then, a number of important foundations had been laid. The major British denominations were all present, with the rudiments of organisation and some buildings in place. There was a small body of clergy, some of whom were very able, and who made notable contributions to the development of Australia. Marsden not only laid the basis for a strong Evangelical tradition, he also demonstrated the very best farming methods of the day. Lang had shown the importance of religious equality before the law and pioneered a long tradition of Christian involvement in education, public life and letters, even if his political radicalism found few imitators. Polding took his Catholic flock into equality with Protestants.

CHAPTER TWO:

Christianisation of Australia 1836–1901

The years from the Bourke Church Act of 1836 which subsidised stipends and the erection of church buildings and the similar act in Van Diemen's Land in 1837, until the discovery of gold, were marked by rapid expansion and the establishment of ecclesiastical government which remained little changed for the rest of the century.[1] By 1850, church accommodation had increased almost five times above what was available in 1836, despite the fact that the population had only increased one and a half times. There were several reasons for this, not least the backlog of need, especially outside the more closely settled areas. The population was assumed to be broadly Christian, so that when facilities for worship and clergy were provided, it would be possible to organise viable congregations quite rapidly. Given those assumptions the major beneficiaries of the Government subsidies—Anglicans, Methodists, Presbyterians and Roman Catholics—sought to ensure that they expanded rapidly, to prevent others attracting their potential adherents.

There were several unintended consequences of this bold experiment in plural establishment. The Anglicans were the major winners, for they had a higher proportion of the substantial families and could more readily raise the money needed to qualify for subsidies, especially with the help of their Societies. Roman Catholics and Methodists asked that aid be more precisely related to the population proportions of the colony, which made Bishop Broughton uneasy, for Catholic priests were much more economical than his clergy. The smaller groups who were either opposed to state aid, like Congregationalists, Baptists and some Presbyterians, found it hard to establish themselves outside the major towns. Those which found it difficult to raise the qualifying money became even more marginal.

The subsidies were channelled through the official church bodies and leaders. It soon became clear that this gave them power to give or withhold, which could disadvantage those who did not see eye to eye with the 'establishment'. That was made plain to Lang when he returned from Scotland in 1836 with a number of ministerial recruits, with whom he hoped to outnumber his opponents. To his chagrin, he found that they were not eligible for aid under Bourke's Act. He formed the separate Synod of New South Wales. Anglicans were likewise uneasy that Broughton's episcopal powers had too little restraint, and Bishop Nixon certainly had no hesitation in using his control of patronage to disadvantage Evangelical clergy in Tasmania.

Denominational Rivalries

There was also a sharpening of denominational identity, without the pattern of common schooling with which Bourke had hoped to counter precisely such a possibility. Such sectarian rivalries were heightened by the emergence of the Tractarian movement in the Church of England after 1833, and the defection of two clergy to Rome in Sydney in 1848, which led other Protestants within and outside the Church of England to be extremely suspicious of ritual innovations. The success of Mrs. Chisholm's immigration schemes and the appalling poverty in post-famine Ireland, led to an influx of Irish that brought Lang into print with a vitriolic tract, *The question of questions* (1841). He asked his readers whether they wished to see the Protestant character of the colony disappear. These issues naturally flowed in to swell the already turbulent currents of politics in the two eastern colonies. Broughton's role in the Legislative and Executive Councils was a genuinely constructive one, ranging over a wide spectrum of issues, but he was suspected of secretly influencing government policy in favour of his own church. While colonial politicians had only limited power, the number of elected members in the Legislative Council expanded. The election of Lang from Port

Phillip Bay in 1843 ensured that discussion of religious and sectarian issues could not be excluded.

Governors and civil servants were uncomfortable in dealing with religious issues. Not only did they lack expertise in matters ecclesiastical, they were much more vulnerable to criticism than in Britain, where the power of the religious establishment kept Nonconformists and Roman Catholics far more firmly subordinate, rather than encouraging notions of equality like the Church Acts did. Coping with the consequences of British disputes was also difficult, for in addition to the factious behaviour of Lang, the Disruption of the Church of Scotland in 1843, over issues of patronage and the relation of State and Church, split Australian Presbyterians hopelessly.[2] Despite their attempts to keep ties both with the Established Church and the Free Church, they were forced to choose, and lose monetary aid and the provision of further ministers, from whichever body they rejected. It was an agonising decision for the Rev. William Hamilton at Goulburn, whom Lang cuttingly dismissed as Mr. Facing-Both-Ways, because of his desire to prevent division over a set of issues which were quite unrelated to Australia. Hamilton went out into a kind of Presbyterian Independency, connected with none of the fractious splinter groups, before moving to Victoria.

There were also serious problems in settling the matter of education, which all Christians agreed was crucial to their future and to the well-being of the colonies' youth. Broughton and Polding were convinced that the only form of education which would provide a satisfactory foundation for moral integrity and citizenship was integrally related to worship and doctrine in their respective churches. The problem was that many Protestants had serious objections to public money from their taxes being used to aid Catholic schools and inculcate what they regarded as Roman error. Others were quite unprepared to support Broughton's proposals, which appeared to entrench Anglican privilege in an unacceptable way. Governor Gipps' attempts to cut through this division by establishing schools in which the Bible was taught but not doctrine, while allowing the Catholics to keep their schools, proved unacceptable. The result was a dual system of government schools and denominational schools which began in 1848 and was extended to Victoria in 1850 and to Queensland in 1859, when they were separated from New South

Wales. As a result, the major churches gained a further accession of political influence and social power, which differed from the British pattern at a number of points. Whether they would be able to use their opportunities in a way which justified the trust placed in them remained to be seen.

Many ministers and their laity were strongly optimistic about the possibilities of building a new society in the south. The Rev. T. Q. Stow, an influential Congregational minister in Adelaide drew some interesting parallels with New England and looked for a third world

> forming under the brilliant lights of expanded science, the rapid processes of modern improvements, the surprising impulse of modern commerce, the meliorations of widely extended philanthropy, the awakened and gathered energies of the Church of God; and further still we see worn-out and decayed portions of the old world renewed, re-animated and re-adorned. In proportion to the sublimity of our position, and our consciousness of occupying it, is our accountability.

To bring that about Stow advised taking a proper political responsibility and infusing "a stern morality, a long cherished philanthropy, the spirit of liberal politics, a pacific temper, an attachment to order, and a conscientious obedience to constituted authority".[3]

Such optimism was especially strong in the colonies of South Australia and Port Phillip Bay, where the constraints and disadvantages of convict labour were absent. It was in South Australia that hopes of creating a new kind of Christian society burned brightest.[4] The Dissenters, who made up a significant proportion of the settlers there, were determined that they would not be subject to the oppression and discrimination from an Established Church which they had known in Britain. Though they were saddled with an Anglican Colonial chaplain, the Rev. C. B. Howard was a firm Evangelical. Holy Trinity Parish, which he founded, has carried that banner to the present. Initial optimism about the advantages of the voluntary system for religion and education was dashed by the hardships of the early years, but when Governor Gawler attempted to put a most modest sum of two and a half thousand pounds on the estimates in 1846, he was strongly opposed by Baptists and Congregationalists. The general feeling in the colony was such that, at the elections of 1851, state aid was a central issue and one of the first acts of the new parliament was to abolish the grant. As well as a strong dissenting tradition in this colony, there was a further strand added by the migration of Prussian Lutherans in 1838, who were determined to retain their heritage, despite the attempt of their government to push them into a union with the Reformed Church.

The religious demography of the 19th century has proved very enduring. Australia has not experienced the seismic impact of a succession of revivals like the United States, or the regional dominance of particular churches. Until recently, Anglicans have been the largest group, followed by Roman Catholics, with interesting variation between states. Methodists were stronger in South Australia than anywhere else, as were Congregationalists and Baptists. Presbyterians were strongest in Victoria, with formidable influence in education, professions and farming. Roman Catholics were especially strong in parts of rural New South Wales and Victoria, as well as strongest in Queensland, and least strong in South Australia.[5] Anglicans formed a tacit establishment in all states, drawing both strength and weakness from that status.

Common Christianity

Many of the Church of England's adherents sat lightly to their formal religious duties and had the lowest church attendance of any of the churches, followed by Presbyterians, who had a different legacy of establishment. And despite the overt sectarian rivalry, the bush could be a great leveller and unifier. The Anglican Bishop of the Riverina noted that infrequent bush services "are valued and well attended. Rarely does anyone of any class stay away because of belonging to another body of Christians." Nor was that just a view from the top. Mark Hammond, a miner, and later a politician, remembered the church at Lower Turon, used by all denominations and built by public subscription.[6] Similar little churches are still to be found in many rural districts, as a reminder of a kind of community Christianity which transcended sectarian rivalries, real though they were.

A common Protestantism seemed to many lay people a practical reality which could be vital to community well-being. At the start of

1882 a group of Anglicans in Gladstone, Queensland, unable to raise the money for a parson of their own, negotiated with Presbyterians to invite a Wesleyan minister to do duty in both churches and to visit all Protestants in the district.[7] Such lay initiative was often responsible for obtaining a minister, or holding a network of Christians together for many years, when ministries were brief and troubled. One of the most notable examples of this was Henry Trigg in Perth, who kept a Congregational presence alive by cottage meetings and then founded a small chapel in 1846 where he administered the sacraments till 1852. A troubled ministry led to the cause collapsing, until Trigg reopened the chapel in 1860. That was to be the forerunner of Trinity Church, which under the Revs. E. J. Dunstan and W. R. Kench grew to a congregation of over nine hundred by the end of the century.[8]

Other lay initiatives that conformed to English patterns included the foundation at Hagley of a parish church in 1856 on the Dry estate in Tasmania, with a generous glebe and four hundred pounds stipend, which was given to Sir Richard's clergyman brother. Mr. Justice Lutwyche in Queensland similarly gave land and building for a parish where three successive members of the Osborne family ministered. As a good lawyer, he had a most interesting congregational compact drawn up, committing the signatories to financial support of both the minister and fabric. Even more interestingly, there were four women on the Parochial Council in 1895–96, which did not happen again for eighty-five years.[9]

Popular religion did not always conform to clerical definition. While many of Australia's early migrants were from humble origins, they included many with great natural ability, who were able to use their gifts in the more open-textured Australian communities to achieve a degree of wealth, position and responsibility which would never have been possible in Britain. Their generosity was very important for the expansion and consolidation of the church and its schools, even if Broughton found that he could not count on the support of the landed groups in his diocese for all his goals. The Morts in Sydney and the Clarkes in Melbourne were important Anglican benefactors; Victorian Presbyterians were helped by the Chirnsides and Francis Ormond; Methodism owed much to Ebenezer Vickery and his family in New South Wales, while Victoria's Walter Powell and Aaron Danks showed how major donors could grow from humble beginnings. In Tasmania, William and Mary Ann Gibson helped to erect at least fifteen Baptist churches and brought out sixteen graduates from Spurgeon's College in London.[10] The energies that went to the making and losing of large fortunes were not always a blessing to the church, for givers expected value for money and a degree of control that some clergy found unnerving. Bishop Thomas of Goulburn found that the promised gifts to found the diocese were likely to be withheld because his Evangelical reputation clashed with the more High Church perceptions of the influential Campbell family.[11]

Self Government

Presbyterians and Dissenters were used to exercising constitutional responsibility in church government at all levels, but it was a novel experience for Anglicans and Wesleyans.[12] While not all laity had time or inclination for Synods and Conferences, compared with the possibilities of local and state government which emerged after the granting of responsible government to most of the colonies in the 1850s, it must be remembered that Australian Anglicans and Wesleyans were also embarking on their first attempts at self-government. The British Wesleyan Conference devolved most of its authority in 1855, even permitting laymen to vote in the Conference here, except on ministerial matters, long before the same privilege was granted in Britain.

For Anglicans, there was a similar process in the newly established dioceses after 1850. Broughton saw the importance of some lay involvement in church government, to balance the powers of Parliament, for he had a high sense of the Church, as well as shrewd political judgement. The Sydney meeting of Bishops from the Australasian colonies in 1850 may have had questionable legality, in the strict sense, but its importance for the development of Anglicanism was immense. It enabled the bishops to explore possibilities of co-operation, especially in missions, to define certain areas of doctrine and to talk over forms of synodal government. Selwyn, Short, Nixon, Tyrrell and Broughton had all been deeply influenced by the High Church or Tractarian ethos and were committed to freeing the Church of England from an Erastian dependence of the State.

There was sharp reaction from laity in Hobart and Adelaide to the agreements reached by the bishops.[13] They feared that episcopal and clerical authority was to be developed in a way which drastically weakened the rights of the laity. Three solutions emerged to the need for a self-governing Church of England in Australia, even if there was no desire to weaken the nexus which was believed to make that church here legally a part of the United Church of England and Ireland. In Adelaide and Newcastle, synodal authority was established by consensual compact, without reference to parliament except in matters of property. In Melbourne, Bishop Perry was able to secure legislative enactment in 1854, and also meet Broughton's fear of lay participation which might lead in a Presbyterian direction. Intensive discussions in England ensured that the Victorian Act received Royal Assent in December, 1855, after it was shown that Royal Supremacy was not endangered. This act provided important precedents for South Africa and Canada and at a later date for the Church in England itself.

In New South Wales, attempts to pass a parliamentary act proved to be politically impossible, and finally an Enabling Act was passed for Sydney in 1866, which clarified the status of property, while underlining the authority of the diocese, rather than the province. It was not all Bishop Barker had wanted, but it was enough. The cherished nexus with the Church of England and its formularies was maintained without any legal doubts threatening property or historic Protestantism. Those concerns, in a series of different ecclesiastical and political climates, have remained in Sydney. A significant number of important and able laity shared in synod deliberations in all the dioceses, giving decisions real public weight, without undermining episcopal or clerical authority. For the first time in well over a century, Anglican clergy were given a constitutional role in synodal government, which far surpassed what had been lost in the disappearance of the Convocations of Canterbury and York under the Stuarts.[14] This has done much to ensure that episcopacy in Australia has been exercised in a conciliar way, substantially different from the English patterns. Broughton gave up his political role in 1846. Australian bishops henceforth were to exercise their public authority as leaders of an important voluntary society, which did not depend on the Crown or parliamentary authority. That in turn made them far more accessible and sensitive to clerical and lay opinion in their dioceses and community. This gave the Church of England here a very real spiritual authority, even if its public role was steadily to shrink and assume forms unfamiliar to English observers. This change was not a compromise with public godlessness, or a rejection of Christianity. It was a response to pluralism and political change, which made older patterns inappropriate, even if it was at the cost of entrenching diocesan autonomy in Australia.

Many Anglican bishops were unmistakably upper class. Some clergy maintained the status of a gentleman, or at least mixed as the equals of many in the professions. Yet the link with wealth and privilege was decisively broken, for in the 1850s and 1860s the massive influx of miners, new patterns of wealth and, above all, the extension of the franchise and the democratising of the lower houses in the colonies made such traditional kinds of religious authority less and less relevant in Australia. In the cities, and in some towns and rural parishes, with wealthy donors, clergy houses were distinctly upper-class. In the bush it was very different. Clergy there roughed it with the rest. Few parishes and congregation had the kind of endowments which removed the need for unremitting attention to money raising, for payment of stipends and the running expenses of the congregation. That further democratised ministry. Those who found that undignified either went hungry, or returned to Britain.

There were many problems over the respective roles of clergy and laity in the holding of property. Such disputes, which are a common feature of migrant churches in the years before canonical and legal procedures are established, have vexed all the churches in Australia. The dealings of Therry and Conolly caused Polding great problems, as did the schemes of Lang in Presbyterian courts. Few managed the financial achievement of Father Backhaus in the Catholic diocese of Bendigo, whose acumen left that diocese one of the best-endowed in Australia.[15] The Anglican glebe lands of Sydney were slow to yield much income, but they and the gifts of Thomas Moore have been very significant in the twentieth century.

Land grants for cemeteries could be a serious source of contention, especially when Anglicans were restrictive about the public use of cemeteries in their control, as was common in England.[16] There was sharp controversy in Adelaide in 1849 when the Governor conveyed fifteen out of twenty-one acres, in a formerly public cemetery, to the Church of England. In the cities, the general cemeteries had areas allocated to denominations, making Australia many years ahead of England in ensuring fair use of burial grounds. The English Burials Act was not passed until 1880. Marriages were also a source of tension, because of the way in which some Anglican clergy interpreted ecclesiastical and statute law. State governments were reluctant to move in such a sensitive area. In South Australia, the Marriage Act of 1867 put all churches on an equal footing. These modifications of establishment in the name of religious equality before the law were not easily won.

Styles of Evangelism

The impact of mineral discoveries on the newly-established colonies was important politically and religiously. The discovery of copper in 1844 in South Australia brought Cornish miners, with a strong Bible Christian revival tradition, which proved to be important also in Victoria, once the alluvial gold was worked out and underground mining developed. Gold in New South Wales and Victoria brought in an enormous influx of miners, who helped to treble Australia's population by 1861. Later rushes in Queensland and Western Australia had the same impact and sorely tested the leaders of all the churches, who had somehow to find men and money for the churches and schools that were suddenly necessary. Such needs could not be provided even with government aid, because the populations were so mobile and the needs too massive. The letters of Broughton and Perry are eloquent testimony to the strain they felt. The theme is repeated in the correspondence of Bishop Parry of Perth in the 1890s, as he sought desperately to finance and recruit clergy.[17] Bishop Stanton in North Queensland had eight clergy for 300,000 square miles and likened recruiting to filling a sieve. Yet by 1883 he had built up a modest endowment and even produced a simplified service book for the bush.

Other churches did not have the Anglican requirements about endowments before dioceses could be established. Creating viable congregations and ministry for a mobile population whose first priority was wealth in this world, rather than salvation in the next, significantly modified patterns of authority, education and recruitment of clergy. Even before the discovery of gold in Victoria, Perry had experimented with the use of lay readers equipped with sound piety and tough constitutions to minister to bush communities. After some study, they were ordained and helped to fill the yawning gaps in pastoral care. Graduate clergy were a much lower proportion here than in Britain and the Colonial Clergy Act of 1819 sanctioned a lower standard of education for Anglicans, on the condition that such clergy did not expect to return to Britain to a secure cure of souls.

Methodists were best placed to meet these new demands. Lay preachers like Jimmy Jeffrey of Ballarat, could edify and convert without the cultural gaps that sometimes hindered communication between clerical gentlemen and the lower orders. Anglicans and Presbyterians soon realised that their people were placing a new value on practical piety, rather than traditional university education. Many young men of humble background and limited education had opportunity to prove themselves effective ministers in the rough schools of the bush and the diggings, imparting a pragmatic character to Australian ministry which has deeply affected all the Protestant churches.

Methodism of various kinds increased its proportion of the population from 5.63% to 13.36% between 1851 and 1901 by its combination of lay preachers, class meetings and circuits and a vigourously evangelistic ethos, as well as the leadership of dynamic clergy like Daniel Draper, the builder of Wesley Church, Melbourne.[18] While Australian Methodism did not grow as rapidly as its North American counterparts, its development was striking and there were local stirrings of revival which deeply affected many local communities. The records of these make fascinating reading, for they help the historian to reconstruct the ways in which men and women discovered the miracle of personal transformation. The language describing such experiences may appear very stylised, but the conversionist tradition put down very deep roots in Protestantism, which have endured strongly into the twentieth century.

Professional evangelists, invited and uninvited, came to help in the work of conversion, beginning with "California" Taylor in 1865, and including women like Mrs. E. Baeyertz and Mrs. M. Hampson, both of whom caused something of a sensation, because they were such a departure from normal roles for women within the churches. There were also a number of Bible Christian women evangelists, the most notable of whom was Serena Thorne. After her marriage to the Rev. Octavius Lake, she continued to have a very important role in many good causes in South Australia, not least temperance. This tradition of evangelism testified to the importance placed on personal salvation and the need for this ministry in local churches. There were some local evangelists who achieved a considerable repute, like the Presbyterian Rev. John MacNeil, but it was normally an outsider who was expected to revive the flagging spiritual energies.[19] Roman Catholics had their own style of such renewal, with the preaching of the Redemptorists. Throughout the various families of Protestantism, such evangelistic preaching found many imitators, especially among lay preachers and home missionaries, who were such an important adjunct to regular ministry in remote or difficult areas. The impact of the Grubb Mission of 1891 in shaping key Sydney clergy like R. B. S. Hammond and laity like E. P. Field, a lawyer and evangelist, has proved to be very enduring, not to mention renewal of missionary enthusiasm.[20]

Evangelism was seen as one of the most effective ways of asserting the social control of Christianity over the rebellious and wayward, and establishing the local church firmly at points of tension and conflict in Australian society. There were a number of battlefronts. The churches, through their members and some of their leaders, were active in seeking to shape public opinion and the activities of legislators. A number of Christians, lay and clerical, owned and edited local and urban newspapers in addition to the strictly denominational monthlies and weeklies which were often influential. Congregationalists were especially active. John West was a notable editor for the *Sydney Herald* and Barzillai Quaife wrote for *The Empire*. The Rev. G. S. Evans was the editor of *The Herald* in Melbourne in the 1850s and 1860s. In Brisbane, the Rev. G. Wight was involved with the *Daily Guardian,* while C. H. Buzzacott in Queensland, ran a chain of small-town papers. In Adelaide, *The Register* and *The Advertiser* had a strong Christian flavour. In Melbourne, the Syme brothers, who had been educated for the Congregational ministry, found a wider platform through *The Age. The Christian Messenger,* which began in Brisbane in 1883, was purchased by the Rev. Dr. Robert Dey in 1891, who by a series of takeovers in other cities established the first national Christian paper, the *Australian Christian World,* which lasted until 1952. In Perth, *The West Australian* was owned and edited by a dedicated Anglican, Winthrop Hackett, whose generosity in the next century was to make possible the University of Western Australia's fine buildings. It was hardly surprising that while such influence could counter the impact of *The Bulletin* and other radical papers, some Christians were anxious by the end of the century about the way in which the press was rivalling the pulpit as a shaper of opinion. Religion's importance was underlined by extensive reporting in both metropolitan and local papers.

Shaping Society

Since many politicians were associated with the churches, they took the creation of a Christian society very seriously, even if the shape did not always correspond to clerical definitions. The political changes that followed the grant of responsible government in the 1850s, and the widening of the franchise, seriously weakened the power of the more conservative allies of the churches. Nowhere was that more clearly seen than in the debates over state aid to churches and denominational schools.[21] The liberal radicalism of Lang, and many who had been Dissenters in England or Voluntaryists in Scotland, proved a natural ally of the more secular liberalism and radicalism which sought to assert public control over education and to reform legal and social anomalies in the name of personal freedom.

Though denominational schools were very numerous and the churches influential politically, there were serious anomalies in state aid, and limitations in the quality of the education offered in the churches' schools. Education needed to be improved and extended if Australia was to become the land of liberty and progress many of its inhabitants desired. Denominationalism was increasingly seen as an obstacle to national education. In state after state, an alliance of radicals and liberal Christians ended both state aid and church schools. Western Australia was the last to fall into line in 1896, but what began in 1851 in South Australia became a common pattern in all the colonies. Designed to end sectarian division, this reform in fact entrenched it, for the Roman Catholic hierarchy fought unyieldingly for parish schools as an essential expression of the faith. At times it was a bitter struggle and the rhetoric on both sides was to inflame public debate on education for another century.[22]

Such a deep-rooted conflict was in part a conflict of visions about Australia. Was it to be Protestant, or was a new religious pluralism, which gave Catholic conscience equal status, to be the direction of the future? There was also a non-religious vision of Australia, expressed by the imprecise words 'secular' and 'non-sectarian'. It was some time before it became clear that some advocates of the secular society were divided between those who were liberal and Christian, and those who were liberal and anxious to diminish the public role of religion, and reducing it to a matter of private choice.

Fierce debates about the sanctity of the Sabbath, and reform of marriage law, were the first significant challenges to the churches as the arbiters of moral judgement.[23] Debates on reform of the liquor industry and gambling at the racing tracks showed even more clearly how deeply the churches were divided about the solution of moral problems, and the ways in which society should be Christianised. For some, there could be no compromise with what they saw as moral evil, even in the smallest way, without inviting the judgement of God in natural disaster and social division. That style was especially associated with the coalition of Evangelical Protestants waging war on the drink and gambling evils. Evangelists like Matthew Burnett and Henry Varley insisted on total obedience to the Word of God as they interpreted it and linked authentic conversion with adoption of a particular lifestyle, which was readily caricatured by cleverly anti-clerical journalists as wowserism, without any credit being given for the work many Christians did for those whose lives had been ruined by alcohol abuse and other destructive forms of behaviour.[24]

'Temperance' became identified with total abstinence from alcoholic drinks and censoriousness, leaving many of those who were genuinely temperate, and saw no harm in an occasional drink or flutter at the races, determined to keep their freedom. Though some victories were won by the hard-liners, by regulation of the liquor trade and racing industry, Australians generally opted for some liberty of choice, supported by important sections in the Anglican, Presbyterian and Roman Catholic Churches who rejected, on principle, legislation for compulsory righteousness.

Such Christians pushed other strategies as more compatible with a Christian society with no established church. One of these was the development of secondary schools, which were of low priority to the state governments. These church schools, which were an interesting blend of English and Scottish models, aimed at the education of Christian ladies and gentlemen. Their beginnings were modest and their finances precarious for the rest of the century, but the quality of many of their heads and staff, has been one of the most important influences the churches have had on the shaping of Australians. They were complemented by Church-related university colleges, a disproportionate number of whose former students have been political, religious, professional and business leaders. They have deeply influenced secondary and university education, though they have also been captive to the ethos of the clientele they served. Another aspect of the importance of the ethos of Australian Christianity can be seen in the hospitals, orphanages, refuges and other caring institutions established in this period by religious orders, individuals and voluntary societies.

Debates on Dogma

Another important area of debate about a Christian society that was challenged was that of the authority to be given to religious dogma, over against the authority of reason and science.[25] For the pious and the conservative there was no problem. Reassertion of past dogma was all that was needed, or perhaps a cautious change on the boundaries of Christian faith. The Roman Catholic bishops were adamant that there could be no compromise with liberalism, indifferentism and various forms of infidelity, which they believed went back to the Reformation. Anglo-Catholics in the Church of England also argued for a reassertion of Catholic authority and a quality of worship which remedied the defects of mere

Protestantism. Their success in capturing most of the dioceses outside Sydney and Melbourne indicates something of their appeal, while the Bush Brotherhoods founded in Queensland in the late 19th century and spreading to many other dioceses of the Church of England were one of the most imaginative answers to the pastoral problems of distance and isolation.[26] The number of their members who became bishops in the twentieth century did much to ensure the continuing impact of this tradition, especially in dealing with some of the effects of unrestrained capitalism in the cities and countryside. They preached and taught an ethic tempered by a mild form of socialism.

In Sydney, Bishop Barry attempted to deal with the problems of doubt and unbelief in the 'eighties by fostering apologetic lectures. Bishops Perry and Moorhouse had remarkable impact in dealing with such issues in Melbourne. Moorhouse's crowded addresses in the Town Hall in the 1880s were long remembered for their intellectual power and spiritual depth. But it was in the Presbyterian Church of Victoria that the issues were most sharply felt. Charles Strong, the cultured and incisive minister of Scots Church invited Mr. Justice Higinbotham to deliver a lecture on "Science and Religion" in 1883. It was a thoughtful and eloquent address, which frankly faced some of the reasons why the old dogmas no longer had their ancient power for church members. Higinbotham's views caused a sensation and a mini-industry sprang into action, to refute him by lectures and booklets. Strong was already suspect among his ministerial brethren for his views on Scripture and Atonement, and though his enemies were unable to bring him to trial for heresy, the discreditable tactics they used impelled Strong to resign. He founded the Australian Church, which included many of Melbourne's elite, where until his death in 1942 he continued to show one of the sharpest social consciences in Australia.[27]

In Adelaide, Miss Catherine Helen Spence had reached her own decision about her family Presbyterianism, and its intellectual and ethical limitations, by becoming a member of the Unitarian Church and a regular preacher. In Brisbane, a remarkable United Free Methodist Minister, W. Osborne Lilley, built up a large congregation by his liberal and evangelical re-interpretation of traditional doctrines. He appears to have been the only minister able to convert

Free-thought lecturers. Lilley also campaigned actively for better sanitation, for the reintroduction of the Bible into state schools and pioneered better relations among the major Protestant churches, as well as being a prolific journalist and close to the socialist William Lane. Methodists appear to have been better placed than any other denomination to accept some of the emphases of theological liberalism, because many of its leading ministers combined appreciation of a more liberal theology with an undiminished fervour for the salvation of souls by evangelism. E. H. Sugden, the Master of Queen's College in Melbourne, had an international repute as a Wesley scholar, but also was very well read in contemporary Methodist theology. Many of the leaders of Methodism in Victoria and other states were deeply influenced by their studies in the Theological Institution at Queen's. In South Australia, other strands of that liberalism were seen in the careers of Hugh Gilmore and Walter Howchin.[28]

Uplifting the Poor

The other side of Methodist adaptability was shown in the development of the Central Methodist Mission in Sydney by W.G. Taylor from 1884. He creatively adapted British and American models of ministry to the urban poor and broke out of Methodist reliance on itinerant ministry, which was both a strength and a weakness. Not only did he revive the York Street church, which was on the verge of closure, because its residential base had been moving to more attractive suburbs, he also engaged in evangelism which was as daring as that of the Salvation Army, which arrived in 1880. He built a whole network of service agencies and was pushed by a determined young woman called Laura Francis to found an evangelical sisterhood in 1890, which offered young women an opportunity to minister, available nowhere else in the Wesleyan church. (Anglicans in Sydney had already established a deaconess ministry in 1886. Presbyterians followed in 1897). Taylor's critics foresaw the introduction of auricular confession next, as part of this move to Rome, but the number of converts to old fashioned evangelism gradually won the doubters over. He was paid the supreme compliment of imitation by Melbourne, where the Rev. A. R. Edgar of Wesley Church adopted similar methods from 1893, but with a more radical edge. He denounced sweating and served on Wages Boards as part of his commitment to the exploited Methodists in industry, as well as helping those thrown out of work by the crash of the nineties which stripped away the facade of "Marvellous Melbourne" to display a mass of misery with uncomfortable similarities to the slums of the old world.[29]

The evident economic injustices of unregulated capitalism led the Presbyterian elder, Sunday School Superintendent and lay preacher of Creswick Presbyterian Church, W. G. Spence, to band workers into unions for improved conditions and wages, rather than relying on preaching and education to change the world. He became one of the men most hated by employers in Australia, many of them fellow Presbyterians, but the Australian Workers Union, which was the final result of his organising genius, has continued. Many Christians distanced themselves from anything resembling socialism, and sought social reform by preaching reconciliation and conversion, with studious vagueness about particular reforms. It was not surprising that the workers on the receiving end of poor housing, poor wages, poor conditions and then unemployment with no buffer but private charity, sought more satisfying alternatives outside the ambit of the churches. In so doing, they caused considerable concern to church leaders who noted falling percentages of attendance.

The churches were still very influential at the end of the century, but the small part they played in the process of federation was a sign of a new situation for which they were not well prepared, despite the achievement of federal union by the Presbyterians in 1901 and by Methodists in 1902.[30] Anglicans had formed a General Synod in 1872, but none of these federal bodies had adequate resources to deal with federal issues that involved more than consultation. Overseas visitors like Dr. R. W. Dale of Birmingham, commented favourably on the vitality of the Australian churches compared with those in Britain and Europe, though there was less sign of the energy and willingness to do new things which characterised sections of American Protestantism. But migrant churches had put down deep roots very quickly and modified the godlessness and corruption of the convict era and British urban society with considerable success.

There was one area of almost total failure—the continued destruction of Aboriginal societies and the inability to control or redeem the violence and dispossession that characterised most white settlement. In no area does the cultural helplessness of successful churches stand more starkly revealed. Here and there were modestly successful missionary attempts to protect what seemed a dying race, accompanied by attempts to break down what remained of Aboriginality by education and civilisation. The Lutheran mission in Central Australia, Bishop Salvado's work at New Norcia, the work of the Moravians in Victoria, or the work of Father Duncan MacNab in Queensland and Daniel Mathews at Maloga showed that white compassion was not dead, but that paternalism to "the child race" was rampant. Anglican and Catholic bishops might plead for compensation and warn of retribution for shed blood, but they went unheard.[31] The fate of the Rev. J. B. Gribble in West Australia in the 1880s exposed the realities of racism in a way that few other cases can. Invited there in 1885 by the Bishop of Perth, his exposure of virtual slavery in the Carnarvon district, led to threats against his life, betrayal by the Committee he worked for and finally his return east, a broken man after losing a libel suit against *The West Australian* which called him "a lying, canting humbug".[32]

There was nothing in the increasingly numerous theological colleges to prepare ministers for that kind of shattering.[33] The Australian churches had won freedom from the embrace of the State for both partnership and critical distance. Whether they had the resources, spiritual or intellectual, to escape from the embrace of social approval from their own community, or to resist it by a rediscovery of the roots of their message remained to be seen. The new century underlined partnership, not critical distance.

PRESBYTERY OF THE HAWKESBURY

EBENEZER CHURCH, HAWKESBURY RIVER,
NEW SOUTH WALES.

(The oldest church now standing in Australia)

CENTENARY CHAPEL AND MISSION HOUSE, NEW YORK STREET,
ERECTED 1839 REV. J. Mc KENNY, SUPERINTENDENT.

CHAPTER THREE:

Fulfilment of the Kingdom 1901–1945

Many church leaders responded enthusiastically to Federation. Melbourne's S. P. Carey of Collins Street Baptist claimed "It is the greatest political triumph He has won in all the annals of the world."[1] There had also been an animated debate in the Perth Anglican Synod about a proposal to rename the Church of England the Church of Australia, so that Anglo-Saxon Christians could be united. "What would do the utmost to bind them to the Empire and make them feel they were all of one blood would be when they could feel they were all united and belonged to one branch of the Catholic Church of Christ."[2] The exultant Protestant sense of sharing an Imperial destiny was muted by sorrow at the death of Queen Victoria, but many of the funeral sermons preached to commemorate her reign underlined the progress of Christian civilisation and the trust which God had committed to the British race. Roman Catholics were not always included in this vision and the promulgation of their *Ne Temere* decree to tighten discipline on mixed marriages in 1908 was taken by many Protestants to be a re-assertion of Roman claims to temporal power, and a denial of the validity of their marriages. Dill Macky, the fiery Irish minister of Scots Church, Sydney, earlier sought to rouse Protestants to defend their heritage against such aggression, through the Protestant Defence Association which he helped to found in 1901. Dispute over *Ne Temere* in New South Wales lasted until the 1920s.[3]

Yet it was becoming clear to more perceptive Protestant leaders that their vision of Australia was only passively shared by many of their contemporaries. An observer in Sydney claimed that only 10% of Anglicans there worshipped regularly and that only 70% of children eligible were brought for baptism. The gap between census figures and reality was to be underlined even more sharply by the experience of chaplains to the armed forces after 1914. There were similar comments about the situation in Britain and North America.

Even if the Australian churches lacked the depth of theological scholarship and spiritual power among their leaders, which was evident in Britain and the United States, there were still some very impressive churchmen in Australia. Archbishops Donaldson and Clarke of Brisbane and Melbourne returned to England, to give distinguished ecclesiastical leadership there. A.G. Price of St. Mark's College, Adelaide was an example of Anglican lay leadership. Principal A. Harper of St. Andrew's College, Sydney, Sir John McFarland of Ormond College, Melbourne and 'Fighting Larry' Rentoul of the Presbyterian Theological Hall in Victoria were substantial Presbyterian leaders, while Henry Howard and F.A. Norwood of Adelaide both became internationally known preachers in Britain and the United States of America. The great Dr. L. Bevan of Collins Street Independent Church, Melbourne, refused a number of invitations to prestigious overseas churches and exerted a remarkable influence in his adopted city. A self-effacing Margaret Holmes gave notable leadership in the Australian Student Christian Movement and the World Student Christian Federation, one of the many Australians who have enriched the ecumenical movement this century. Robert Harkness of Bendigo who became a composer of hymns and music which won him international acclaim, travelled widely as a musical evangelist.[4]

The public impact of the Chapman and Alexander evangelistic campaigns in 1909 was large, and helped to reinforce Protestant confidence that God was bringing an irresistible tide of spiritual renewal to the world through English-speaking Christianity. The great missionary conference in Edinburgh in 1910 and the visits of John Mott, the great student evangelist, to Australasian universities deeply influenced many students and led them to missionary service overseas or to dedicated service in Australian churches and communities. Churches were centres of educational, social, sporting and cultural activity and provided charitable care unmatched by the state or secular organisation. Perhaps the Rev. F.B. Boyce was more than a touch triumphalist in his 1905 book *What the Church of England has done for New South Wales,* but a study of parish histories can very quickly show the local impact of the churches. On the frontiers of settlement, ministers could have major influence. The work of the Baptist missionary William Kennedy in West Australia was a reminder of that, as was the remarkable ministry of another Baptist, F.J. Wilkin, in northern Victoria.

Church leaders still devoted an enormous amount of energy to attacking the influence of the liquor industry. That was undoubtedly helped by the impact of women's suffrage and the work of the Women's Christian Temperance Union.[5] Indeed hatred of alcohol had reached such heights in the evangelical churches that by 1914 many had dropped the use of communion wine, for various other decoctions—a remarkable example of how ideology could distort obedience to the Scriptures. American example, and anxiety about infection from such diseases as TB, also led a number of churches to replace the common cup by individual glasses for communion services in the first decade. Defence of racial purity, attacks on promiscuity and contraception and awful warnings against the hazards of self-abuse reflected concern about the need to populate the continent, lest it be taken by Asiatic hordes and lost to Christian civilisation. The idealised picture of Christian womanhood presented in sermons and print underlined commitment to particular views of family life and respectability, which were shared by Catholics and Protestants alike. Archbishop Duhig's advice to young ladies in Brisbane and S.J. Hoban's sermons in the Sydney and Melbourne Central Methodist Missions had much in common in that regard.

A minority of clergy and laity were concerned about the economic and social problems of the urban and rural poor, though theological discussions about socialism did not have the same urgency as they had in the last decades of the previous century. Anglican Church Congresses could be guaranteed to have papers on these subjects, but there was little sign that words were effectively translated into action. The exception was the astonishing ministry of R.B.S. Hammond in Sydney, at St. Barnabas', Broadway. He brought the same commitment to a wide-ranging social ministry of evangelism and service that he had shown when he played football for Essendon and Victoria.[6]

Seeking Reunion

There was also some discussion of the ways in which Christian reunion would enable the Protestant churches to meet the needs of the newly united nation, for which such an influential future was seen. Presbyterians and Methodists dreamed of a united evangelical church and invited Congregationalists to join them. The Presbyterian General Assembly of 1901 issued invitations to form such a church. By 1907 a Basis of Doctrine and a Scheme of Polity had been drafted, using documents from the similar Canadian scheme. The Right Rev. John Meiklejohn, the first Moderator-General, acknowledged the debt Presbyterians had to other denominations, the growth of common interests and recognition of the evils of division. Even more important was his stress on the link of unity with the mind of Christ, and the need to recognise that there were elements of doctrine and polity which were not of front rank importance. These arguments probably did not carry so much weight as the pragmatic arguments, which had been under consideration in confessional reunions—the folly of overlapping, the advantages of co-operation in matters like overseas mission, home mission and theological education, not to mention youth work where Sunday Schools and organisations like Christian Endeavour had already broken down denominational divisions.[7]

The Churches of Christ did not join the negotiations, and Baptists had withdrawn by 1910. A number of Anglican dioceses were interested and the matter came to General Synod in 1905. Meetings were held with Presbyterians in 1906, 1907 and 1909 in St. Paul's Cathedral, Melbourne, but there were important legal and doctrinal difficulties as well as deep aversion among many Anglo-Catholics to any fraternal relation with other denominations. In Queensland, Archdeacon Glennie rejoiced that in thirty-seven years he had never fraternised with clergy of other churches. Even in Evangelical Sydney, there was hostility to exchange of pulpits. When the Rev. R. Eyton from Bathurst holidayed in Sydney and preached in two Presbyterian churches, forty three Sydney clergy wrote a letter of protest to his bishop.[8] Nevertheless, the extent of agreement was large, though Principal Harper sounded warnings over the importance of Presbyterian ordination being recognised. The method of unification was referred to the 1908 Lambeth Conference, but the major sticking point was the legal ruling that the dioceses in Australia were actually part of the Church of England and could not in any way modify her law, only submit to it. Regretfully the Presbyterian Assembly of 1912 agreed that there be no further negotiations with Anglicans until they secured sufficient autonomy to negotiate. That was not to be achieved until the constitution for General Synod was agreed in 1962.

Matters were more promising with Methodists and Congregationists and by 1910 a Basis had been drafted and amended by 1914. However influential Presbyterians in Victoria like Rentoul were opposed, as were Congregationalists like Leyton Richards and Dr. A. Gosman. The Methodists discharged their committee when the 1914 General Assembly had a tied vote and it appeared likely that Presbyterians would be unable to proceed. Yet the outbreak of war underlined for some the importance of proceeding further, and by 1918 a slightly revised Basis was produced. It was voted on in 1920. Congregationalists voted 84%, Methodists 90%, and Presbyterians 60% in favour. There was a very close Presbyterian vote in Victoria. By 1922, when there was another vote, the opposition had increased in the Presbyterian Church—to the point where it was clear that to go ahead would likely split that Church. So negotiations ground to a halt.

Horace Wootton, a Melbourne Congregational layman, convened a meeting of Christians in February, 1913 to explore the possibilities of calling a Congress in August. Some very important work was done at the Congress in exploring sensitive issues and it was a remarkable example of the way a lay initiative could do much to break down misunderstanding. Both these strands of ecumenism included Anglicans and were light years ahead of similar meetings in Britain.

One of the most important consequences of these conversations and negotiations was the formation of the Melbourne College of Divinity in 1910, as an examining, but not a teaching body. In 1904 the Royal Commission on the University suggested that, if a nonsectarian faculty could be appointed, a School of Theology could be included. That evoked violent opposition from some of the staff and graduates, who believed that retaining the secular character of the University was essential for its unity and welfare. The Anglican Synod initially rejected the proposal for such a college, because some still pinned their hopes on an agreement with the University. Other opponents felt that the qualifications of the college would be of little value compared with the possibilities of working for the degrees of the University of London. However, Archbishop Clarke won over the doubters, the Catholic Archbishop Carr did not oppose and a majority was obtained in the Victorian Parliament. One member saw the College as a centre for national ministerial training. "There is no reason we should not have at one of the great centres in Australia, a College of Divinity which would rank with some of the universities that are specially devoted to divinity in Europe."[9]

The College began awarding degrees and diplomas in 1914 and has served Australasia well ever since, providing a model by which Brisbane, Adelaide, Sydney and Perth have all recently set up similar bodies, in which teaching is carried out by associated theological institutions, but the government of the college is vested in officially appointed church representatives. Along with the ecumenically remodelled Australian College of Theology, which had been founded in 1891 by the Anglican General Synod, the Melbourne College of Divinity was a notable piece of pioneering in distance and further education, which did much to help raise the standards of ministerial education.

One other important example of a single-issue ecumenism which bore successful fruit was the campaign to reintroduce the Bible into Queensland's state schools. The movement had begun in the previous century through the work of the Rev. C.O. Lilley, and Bishop Webber, but the key person was Canon D.J. Garland, one of the ablest Anglicans of the century.[10] He was able to overcome the opposition of some Anglo-Catholics to non-denominational Christian teaching, for it became clear that the Catholic Church was quite opposed to denominational teaching in public schools. Garland, who was appointed organiser by the Bible in State Schools League in 1907, speedily built up a very effective coalition and persuaded them to agree on quite specific aims. He won more and more public support by local polls and carefully orchestrated publicity from influential citizens. Resistant politicians, who feared sectarian conflict, had their fears assuaged and irrefutable evidence of majority public support. In 1910 an Act was passed permitting Bible reading in school hours. Garland came very close to pulling off a similar campaign in New Zealand, but that was stopped there with the outbreak of war in 1914. It was a reminder that the churches could in certain circumstances be a very effective lobby, even if their actual influence in public education diminished as the system expanded, and became more professional and bureaucratic. Yet the pioneering initiatives of the churches in education must not be forgotten, least of all Protestant concern for the quality of public education. Though it may seem intrusive to politicians, administrators and teachers defensive of their territory, the churches' interest in and commitment to education has been an important part of Australian history.

Aboriginal Missions

The impact of Federation can be seen in one other area—a renewal of interest in mission to the Aborigines, especially in North Queensland and in the Northern Territory, which was taken over by the Federal Government in 1911. Methodists explored the possibility of opening up a mission and began work in 1916. Anglicans began work there and also expanded into West Australia The Roman Catholics extended into the Kimberleys at Kalumburu; while Father F. X. Gsell, after doing an apprenticeship at Darwin, began work on Bathurst Island in 1911, where he became famous as the Bishop with 150 wives. The Presbyterians in Victoria employed Moravian missionaries to begin work in Queensland at Mapoon in 1891. They extended to Weipa in 1898 and to Aurukun in 1904.[11]

Concerns for evangelism intersected with the aims of native administrators to pacify tribes and to dispose of half-castes. Missionary strategy was still heavily paternalistic and civilising. A. Ward's *Miracle of Mapoon*, published in 1908, is fascinating for the frankness with which it discusses the physical repulsion the missionaries felt for their charges, and the ways in which they sought to break attachment to 'socialist' traditional culture, so that the Gospel of personal responsibility could take root. They accepted the common assumption that there was little likelihood of Aboriginal survival, but believed that strict segregation from white contact was essential, a policy supported by administrators. Pacific Island missionaries were an important addition to the work of the white missionaries, for they were often able to communicate much more effectively and better understand some of the dynamics of Aboriginal society.

There were also a few Aboriginal Christians who showed that it was possible to hope for indigenous leadership. James Noble who was the first Aboriginal to be ordained by any of the churches, became an Anglican deacon in Perth, on 13 September, 1925. He began work with the mission at Yarrabah about 1896 , spent a brief time at Roper River and then after returning to Yarrabah volunteered for Forrest River in West Australia in 1914–32, before returning to Queensland, where he died in 1941. He was clearly a man of great ability, an eloquent speaker with a splendid command of English, an athlete and also deeply versed in Aboriginal custom. It was a tragedy that he was not ordained to the priesthood, to foster the development of an indigenous ministry. Another was (Sir) Douglas Nicholls, who in 1932 committed himself to Christ and, after an outstanding sporting career, became a missionary with the Churches of Christ in 1944, working from the Gore Street Church in Fitzroy, Melbourne. These two men were exceptions, but have become increasingly important as Aboriginal Christians discover their history.[12]

Progress to leadership was to take much longer in the Northern Territory, though the conversion of Harry Foster in 1936 and his nurture by W.A. Long of the Aboriginal Evangelical Fellowship again showed what possibilities responsibility could open up.[13] White attitudes of contempt were difficult for the churches to modify in the outback. Racism continued to have a destructively negative effect throughout the period. The appalling massacre in West Australia near Forrest River, which led to a Royal Commission that reported in 1921, indicated police responsibility for the death of at least eleven and possibly as many as thirty Aborigines. It did not lead to a single prosecution. The involvement of the Rev. Ernest Gribble as a witness was ironic, in view of his father's fate in the previous century. One of the police lawyers alleged that Gribble puffed up blacks and had been a source of great mischief in the Wyndham district.

The churches were not able to persuade government to use interpreters in court, and the miscarriages of justice that resulted are a tragic testimony to cultural insensitivity. That was underlined in the

Northern Territory. There the Anglican and Methodist churches were able to head off a major punitive expedition to Caledon Bay in the early thirties, after the killing of Japanese and white adventurers, and a policeman. A Church Missionary Society party led by the Rev. H. Warren and A. Dyer volunteered to try and bring out those responsible. They succeeded by early 1934.[14] The resulting trial in Darwin underlined the cultural gap between white and black. The sentences were so severe that they provoked an outcry and review, in which the Anglican and Methodist churches played an important part. One of the freed Aboriginals, Tuckiar, disappeared, almost certainly disposed of by Darwin whites who felt he had got off too lightly.

Two Presbyterians combined in 1937 to pioneer a new mission to the Centre at Ernabella. They were the Rev. H. Taylor and Dr. Charles Duguid of Adelaide. The latter was one of the most powerful and effective advocates for Aboriginal people Australia has seen. The Lutheran missions were also reaching a point where significant Aboriginal response showed that far more than dependence was involved. Rather Aborigines were beginning to adopt Christianity on their own terms, without forsaking their own cultural patterns. Independent missionaries like the Schencks at Mt. Margaret in West Australia also demonstrated that there were whites who were prepared to face the hostility and ridicule of their own people to minister to Aborigines. The Schenks were severely hampered by the unscrupulous and bitter opposition of local farmers, who did their best to deprive the mission of its small grant of land. The work of the Pallotine Fathers in North West Australia from 1904 marked a new maturity in missionary understanding of Aboriginal religion and culture, especially through the work of Father E. A. Worms, a notable missionary anthropologist.[15]

Methodists like the Revs. T. T. Webb and W. Chaseling also were moving beyond traditional understanding of missionary work. Both learned from the field work and theory of anthropologists like Sydney's Professor A. P. Elkin, an Anglican priest whose views on Aborigines have had remarkable influence. The result was a genuine attempt to integrate the central convictions of the Christian faith with major patterns of Aboriginal beliefs, rather than assume that conversion was a one-way process. Reading missionary letters and diaries certainly brings out the writers' frailties, but also draws attention to the courage and faith of some very gifted men and women, who gave their lives to this work, at a time when isolation, illness, physical danger and heartbreaking failure were all too common. Such pioneers are a reminder that social and religious transformation do not come easily, and that the interaction of lives is essential.

It is now more obvious that missionary acceptance of some government policies about the treatment of half-castes and the tragic separation of children from parents, so that they could be socialised, created deep personal and social scars. Learning to keep a critical distance from obvious community wisdom is one of the hardest lessons the Churches have had to learn. They cannot cut themselves off from their supporters. They cannot be wholly a reflection of their expectations either. Churches are very dependent on charismatic individuals who open out new possibilities. One of these was a Roman Catholic layman, Francis J. McGarry, whose work among the neglected half-caste children round Alice Springs soon evoked hard-edged racist opposition to his work. That led to the severance of his connection with the parish and great frustration in trying to work within the parameters of administration policy as a civil servant.[16]

Another visionary was John Flynn, whose survey of the spiritual needs of Inland families, led to the foundation of the Australian Inland Mission of the Presbyterian Church and encouraged the later work of the Methodists. By comparison, General Synod in the 1930s was not able to agree to such a national policy, and it was left to S. J. Kirby (later Bishop) to meet some of the pastoral needs of the isolated through the Bush Church Aid Society founded in 1919. Flynn's report enthused the 1912 General Assembly. It was a fascinating blend of economic developmentalism and mythology about the spiritual values of the bush, which he believed could help to purify the nation. Add to that a shrewd practicality, ability to listen and yarn, and above all a capacity to harness the expertise of others and there is the beginning of an explanation of his stature. The development of hospitals, pedal radio and the flying doctor service captured the imagination and generosity of many Australians and New Zealanders. The assistance of Dr. George Simpson of Melbourne and a supportive Assembly Committee was important for the success of his dream, but the quality of the people he attracted was even more significant. Bruce Plowman, the first missionary Flynn engaged, wrote splendid letters to his family and fianceé which give a vivid picture of the rewards, loneliness and frustrations of his work. The mobile ministry of the patrol padres was as innovative as the Bush Brotherhoods had been for Anglicans. It indicated a combination of vision, practicality and Christian compassion which was a distinctive adaptation to the distances of the inland.[17] Flynn worked within white assumptions about Aborigines and though he and Duguid clashed over that, the Inland Mission hospitals provided treatment for Aborigines which governments did not.

Impact of War

The intersection of communal and Christian values was powerfully demonstrated during the First World War. Clergy of the Protestant churches outdid one another in lauding the virtues of patriotism, sacrifice and heroism, suggesting that war would purify and ennoble Australia. The roles of recruiting agent and conveyor of news of death and wounding to families were not easily reconciled, and became more burdensome as the casualty lists lengthened. Charles Strong, of the Australian Church was one of the few clergy to challenge the cult of war and to remind rather deaf believers that Christians had a peace mission. He founded the Sisterhood of International Peace in 1915 and edited the journal *Peacewards* from 1915–42.[18]

The impact of war can be gauged by the memorial chapel in the Anglican Cathedral at Goulburn with its name-covered walls, bearing mute testimony to the human cost of the struggle. While the study of civil religion in Australia is not as advanced as in the United States, the process by which the terrible failure on Gallipoli led to the development of an Anzac ethos, where defeat was transmuted into noble sacrifice for freedom, is a fascinating example of the way Christian themes were laicized, as the Returned Services League rather than the churches controlled the Anzac services, which grew out of the first service in 1916 held by the Queenslander Canon D.J. Garland. These services were the only place where the ecumenism of need and suffering which had been forged in war could be remembered in peacetime. Later attempts by the Anglican Archbishop Head of Melbourne to protest against the omission of prayers which, in his judgement, made Anzac services Christian led to sharp comments by Archbishop Mannix about Protestant insensitivity to the law of the Roman Catholic Church, which forbade sharing in prayers by other Christians.

Chaplains to the forces had begun by keeping official boundaries very strictly, but as the war progressed that became impossible, so many of the chaplains and troops gained a new insight into the convictions of their separated brethren. One of the most perceptive comments on the spiritual issues opened up in the forces was written by an Anglican—Chaplain Kenneth Henderson from Melbourne. His *Khaki and Cassock* stands comparison with any of the books written by British chaplains. He and his colleagues were shaken by the ignorance of Christianity they found, which suggested serious weaknesses in the pastoral and educational work of the Churches. That was to lead Henderson into journalism and religious broadcasting with the ABC. Like others he found great difficulty in reconciling the magnitudes of suffering with traditional theodicy and eschatology. There were few helpful treatments of death and immortality, though Professor R.G. MacIntyre's book made a deep impact.[19]

The social effects of war were enormous. Apart from the strains on families with breadwinners killed or maimed, women tasted the privileges of higher wages and a degree of independence hitherto unknown. The imposition of 6 o'clock closing to help the war effort was to divide the community for a half century and demonstrate Evangelical power to create an atmosphere in which a coalition of interests could push government to action. Profiteering was not so successfully dealt with by moral pressure from the Churches. Christian moral concern still tended strongly to focus on alcohol abuse, gambling and sexual licence. The Churches sought to ensure that recruits were protected from such moral corruption. The tents and huts which they and the YMCA gave provided constructively for their leisure. Many women wore themselves out making comforts for the troops and normal parish activities often took second place to war related efforts.

Sectarian Divisions

The sectarian divisions roused after 1917 by Protestant reactions to the defeat of the conscription referenda were to leave a bitter legacy of mistrust in Victoria and New South Wales, but relations were much less strained in Queensland. There Archbishop Duhig and his people seemed much less threatening and the Anglo-Catholic ethos of the Anglican Church made it less possible for the weaker Methodists and Presbyterians to stoke the fires of sectarianism.[20] Though these social strains could be taken as a sign that ancient loyalties were still very powerful political catalysts, the postwar years saw a substantial weakening of the formal influence of the Protestant churches in matters of both faith and ethics, particularly at the national level. That was due to the inability of the churches to cope with the plurality of views, which made it plain that substantial elements of the common Protestantism were undergoing redefinition.

There are a number of signs of this re-definition and its debilitating effects, not least the increasingly hollowness of the claims of Protestant leaders to speak authoritatively on behalf of their census constituency. Astute politicians were cautious, but the more perceptive noted that the evidence for Churches being able to deliver votes reliably in ballot boxes was ambiguous. In the Church of England the debilitating effect of the failure to reach agreement on a new federal constitution for General Synod showed how deeply Evangelicals and Anglo-Catholics were divided. Both parties entrenched themselves in dioceses, or in semi-independent parishes like St. George's, Goodwood in Adelaide where the Rev P. Wise drove the authorities to distraction by his conscientious disregard of official liturgical order, in the name of obedience to his party vision of worship and social order. That diversity was possible in cities, but in rural dioceses like Wangaratta, the disappearance of Evangelical clergy did not go unnoticed in Sydney, where the battle to safeguard the Protestant heritage of the Church of England was at its sharpest.[21] The combined efforts of the Anglican Church League (a formidable caucus), the leadership of Archbishop Mowll, Principal Hammond and a network of able Evangelical clergy and laity gave the Sydney diocese a status unique in the worldwide Anglican communion. Sydney leadership saw the supremacy of Parliament and law as an essential safeguard for the authority of the Scriptures in the life of the church, over against Anglo-Catholic attempts to 'subvert' that heritage by modifying the Prayer Book and Canon

Law in a Roman direction, and exalting the spiritual authority of the bishops over against the priesthood of all believers.

There were signs of the same division over the increasingly difficult economic and social issues facing the nation, beginning with the challenges of post-war reconstruction and migration. By the late 1920s it was clear that the settlement schemes had been badly conceived and placed impossible burdens on many families, who were quite incapable of turning bush and poor soil into prosperous farms, even if there had been a long boom in agricultural prices. The onset of depression made plain how limited much ecclesiastical thinking was in dealing with the complex issues of social and economic ethics. In Melbourne, the Rev. R. G. Nichols of St. Mark's, Fitzroy, one of the few clergy with a real knowledge of economics, exercised a remarkable ministry in his working-class parish, using film and radio to be Brother Bill to thousands who would have otherwise have been forgotten. From a different Anglican tradition, Father G. K. Tucker began the Brotherhood of St. Laurence. Their diocese found it difficult to cope with this entrepreneurial style, which reached out into many other parishes.[22]

None of the Anglican dioceses were able to develop regional organisations to deal with the massive human needs of the unemployed. Nor were the bishops and senior clergy able to adapt overseas insights in social ethics, with the exception of Bishops Burgmann of Goulburn and Moyes of Armidale. Burgmann was a lonely voice, but his numerous books, pamphlets, articles, addresses and sermons did a little to swing perceptions away from exclusive dependence on the old values of liberalism and individual initiative. Other bishops, clergy and laity showed a fascination with the notion of supra-party government by the wise and the good who could transcend the divisiveness of party politics.

Ideological Challenges

The number of Presbyterians and Methodists who were attracted by the strong leadership of Hitler and Mussolini is sobering, now that the extent of the secret and not-so-secret armies of the twenties and thirties, like the White Guard and the New Guard is better known. The fear of Socialism and Communism was very deep, but the most potent answer to assuage those anxieties came from a young law graduate of Italian origins—B. A. Santamaria—who became the protege and confidant of Archbishop Mannix.[23] There were other Roman Catholic laity involved in the beginnings of the National Secretariat of Catholic Action in 1937 and the cluster of organisations which fed into it, but Santamaria was a dominant force because of his incisive mind and his remarkable grasp of issues. He had a substantial part in the drafting of the Catholic hierarchy's annual statements on social issues, which for comprehensiveness and vision left the other Australian Churches far behind, not to mention Catholic churches in other parts of the Empire and North America. Even more important, Santamaria and Mannix were working on plans to end the influence of the Communist Party in the unions and the Labor Party through The Movement.

Santamaria has never been forgiven by those he helped to defeat and it is not yet possible to estimate his significance. His humility about his own personal importance cannot disguise his passionate commitment to theological and ethical truth, based on a vision of a Christian Australia, which made him one of the most influential political and religious figures in the twentieth century, and a Christian layman of world stature, too little known by Protestants. A better example could hardly be found of the way in which migration has both enriched Australia and enabled a person of such ordinary origins to use the opportunities this country provided to make such a notable contribution to his homeland. Other laity in the Protestant churches also made important contributions to reforming the structural defects of Australian society. The Melbourne Methodist, F. O. Barnett, was conventional when he founded the Methodist Babies Home, but highly innovative in the way he attacked the immense problem of appalling housing in inner Melbourne. Accusations of "communism" cost him employment opportunities, but he chose quite deliberately to work for housing reform, rather than gaining personal wealth. The Housing Commission was one of the results.

That kind of Christian influence and vision is an outworking of the Protestant doctrine of vocation. It is not so readily measurable as the activities of politicians, but it contributes immeasurably to what politicians and civil servants see to be possible and desirable. Nor can the historian of the churches in Australia ignore the effect of lay Christian service through business, professions, trade unions, the public service, local bodies, voluntary service and sport. The importance of Christians in wealth creation is not unique. It has had tragic ambiguities and elements of exploitation. But the energy behind the grocery and food empire of Moran and Cato owed much to the deep devotion that led Fred Cato to rise at 4.45 a.m. every day for one and a half hours of prayer and Bible reading, before he undertook the business of the day. The unique co-operative developed by Fletcher Jones, who was deeply influenced by T. Kagawa of Japan, showed the same religious influences as did the Gilbertsons of Essendon, who have for several generations provided lay preachers, service to local government, as well as building one the largest unlisted family companies in Australia.[24] They are all examples of the way in which Christian influences should not be narrowly identified with the leaders and institutions of the Australian churches. Such Christian service may have a rather anonymous quality, in terms of measurable piety, but it has been shaped by deep convictions forgotten by many of the present generation, not least by historians who have a genteel distaste for trade and entrepreneurship.

Mapping the experience of divine grace in worship and private devotions, which lies behind such service, confronts the historian with an almost impossible task in generalising about the relation of liturgy, piety and folk religion. Externally, little changed in the patterns of worship in the major Churches, yet there were signs of an increasingly lay definition of piety, expressed in a number of ways. Many Protestants saw no necessary connection between attendance at worship and commitment to the moral values of their tradition. The cluster of attitudes summed up in the phrase "the right of private judgement" place little value on the Church as a means of grace.

The religious enthusiasm linked with revival campaigns and the Hickson Healing Mission of 1923, plus personal conversion, continued to be an important part of a subculture, obscured by the more liberal and cerebral attitudes of important Protestant clergy like Principal Kiek of Parkin College, Adelaide. Institutionally, it led to the growth of faith missions and Bible colleges and institutes, which were an Australian reflection of the tensions within American Protestantism. Liberal clergy differed from fundamentalist laity committed to past definitions of Protestantism, which seemed to provide a more authentic basis for experience of God than the rational judgements of liberalism. The beginning of pentecostal piety in the Good News Hall at North Melbourne under a former Methodist, Mother Lancaster, in 1909 and in the modest revival at Sunshine in 1916 which led to the foundation of the mother church of Pentecostalism here—Richmond Temple—was another example of fresh currents of religious experience which began in Australian homes, not in response of visiting evangelists.[25]

In Sydney, Mrs. Emily Herman, a Presbyterian who later became an Anglican, wrote perceptive articles for the *Australian Christian World* from 1908 before the First World War, and later published two fine books on prayer and mysticism, which are lonely exemplars and too little known. Bishop Mercer of Tasmania wrote in 1913 on *Nature Mysticism* but without a single reference to the Australian landscape. The deep classical spirituality of some clergy and members of religious orders was inaccessible to the general Christian community. There the Protestant traditions of prayer meetings and quiet times, together with family prayers were beginning noticeably to decline, without any substitute.

Scientific method appeared to offer a more reliable way to personal and social renewal. Samuel Angus, the noted Professor of New Testament in St. Andrew's College, Sydney, attempted to remedy the deficiency by a liberal combination of imitation of Jesus and deep ethical commitment, overlaying his Ulster Presbyterian folk piety. He rejected the emotionalism of mass evangelism. His proposal that there should be a moratorium on such visitors confirmed the evangelical stereotype that liberalism was the enemy of true religion, the more dangerous because it appeared to use familiar language. The attempts to try him for heresy from 1933 on were a sensation.[26] Dr. W. H. Fitchett's *A tattered Bible and mutilated Christ* (1926), did not persuade Methodist leaders to change direction, though some conservative Methodists like Irving Benson, in 1933, professed to find a new spirituality in the Oxford Groups, founded by Frank Buchman.

There was simply no Christian agreement about the foundations needed to prevent Australia sinking into paganism, a fate feared by liberals and evangelicals alike. The dilemma was the more poignant because traditional denominationalism clearly did not have the resources to cope with the challenges posed by ideology, depression and war.[27] Yet ecumenism was too slight and suspect to provide a new context for addressing these issues. A conference held in Newcastle between 6 and 13 September, 1942, was the first to break through Protestant and Roman Catholic barriers in an attempt to explore the role of Christians in a changing world. Dame Enid Lyons and D. Jackson (Roman Catholic), Cumming Thom and Boyce Gibson (Presbyterian), J. W. Burton (Methodist), James Darling, (Anglican) provided a galaxy of insight, which alas did not bear much fruit. The difficulty of moving beyond confessionalism and traditional social and political alignments was nowhere seen more clearly than in the refusal of Protestant leaders to accept Santamaria's invitation to co-operate in transforming Australian perceptions. The Protestant heart was still firmly connected to a liberal circulatory system, but, as the pace of change increased, it was difficult to decide which cultures should shape the translation of the Gospel.

Nor were there enough Australian Christians qualified to wrestle with the political realities created by the Russian Revolution of 1917, the collapse of liberal democracy in Germany and Italy and the evident failure of the League of Nations to deal with mounting international tensions and naked aggression by Japan, Italy and Germany. Nor did the outcome of the Spanish Civil War offer much comfort to those who believed in a rational and democratic society. The outbreak of another global war caught many Australians unaware and exposed the hollowness of much of the inter-war thinking about international affairs in all the Australian churches. Their role in that war was more marginal that it had been twenty-five years before. There was little of the triumphant patriotism of an earlier era and there was slight readiness for the kind of denominational cooperation demanded by war.

The partnership of Methodists and Presbyterians in Darwin, which was the foundation of the later creation of the United Church of North Australia, was a creative departure from their failure to cooperate in Canberra. It would have been unlikely if there had not already been an understanding that Presbyterians would not build a church in Darwin, but rather encourage Methodists to develop a community Protestant Church. That in turn went back to the twenties and the partnership which grew out of the great missionary conference held in Melbourne in 1926.

Ecumenism may have had its limitations, but Methodists and Presbyterians achieved union in Australia long before their British parent bodies did in 1929 and 1933 respectively. And joining hands across the Tweed or Irish Sea was undreamt of. British Christianity was uncompromisingly local and ethnic still, a fact which makes the development of partnership in Australia all the more remarkable, given the geographic difficulties. The churches entered the atomic era with both strengths and weaknesses. A more complex nation and world made the task of influencing and shaping it likely to be far more taxing than hitherto.

BRUNSWICK STREET WESLEYAN SABBATH SCHOOL FITZROY

CHAPTER FOUR:

Towards a Catholic Australia 1945–1988

The period after the end of war in 1945 had many continuities with Christian patterns of witness in the early twentieth century. Church leaders and people alike believed that they were shapers of the nation's conscience and moral values, and gatekeepers against attitudes and practices which would undermine what seemed long-held values.[1] The discovery of the extent of the Nazi massacres of six million Jews and twenty million Slavs, and the sheer inhumanity of the death camps, were a shattering reminder of the human capacity for wickedness. The capacity for societies to shut their eyes and ears to massive corporate evil was a terrible reality for many refugees who came here. The return of so many members of the armed forces from Nazi and Japanese prison camps was a further reminder of human evil and of the cost of war, as well as a tribute to the capacity of the human spirit in men like "Weary" Dunlop (now Sir Edward) to survive overwhelming odds. Few in the churches however, appreciated the implications of the atomic weapons which had brought such a speedy end to the war, and the way their presence was to shape the rest of the century.

The enormous increase in human power to shape the environment was underlined by the extraordinary pace of technological change, progress in the conquest of disease and the capacity of scientists to expand the frontiers of knowledge. It was scarcely surprising that there was a qualified optimism in the Australian scientific community that it would be able to enrich the nation's life. Some, like Sir Mark Oliphant, saw no significant place for religion in the present or the future. The growth of the social sciences since the sixties has further increased optimism about the possibilities of personal and social change, without reference to religion. Few were more eloquent advocates of those views than Mr. Gough Whitlam, a former Prime Minister and the High Court Judge Lionel Murphy. That optimism about change was fed by seemingly unbroken economic progress, where the riches of the continent transformed perceptions in the business and farming communities. Australia seemed to many to offer the kind of limitless frontiers of opportunity which the United States had in the 19th century. The churches also took initiatives which are likely to be as formative as some of the choices made last century.

While these trends had not been so apparent in the 'forties, there was agreement about the need for moral, spiritual and economic change if peacetime was to be more than a rerun of the past. The Christian Social Order Movement led by the Rev. W. G. Coughlan of Sydney had some influence in this rethinking.[2] Many in the churches, who had been deeply disappointed by the failure of the League of Nations, hoped that the United Nations would provide a more realistic forum for international co-operation and the prevention of war. Norman Makin, a South Australian Methodist and federal Labor member, was deeply involved in the United Nations, along with H. V. Evatt whose link with the churches was far more tenuous. Forces' chaplains were actively involved in moral leadership courses, especially for officers, and the common experience of suffering in all ranks had once again underlined that denominational barriers had little social utility when life and death were involved.

Hardly surprising then that the re-emergence of the ecumenical movement and the formation of the World Council of Churches at Amsterdam in 1948 provided new models and context for ecumenical co-operation on a limited basis. The Anglican Primate, Archbishop Mowll of Sydney, attended Amsterdam and was the first President of the Australian Council of the World Council of Churches.[3] At many points, this example of unity was distant from the experience and aspirations of Australian Protestants, but it proved to be increasingly important for the ecumenically minded and for the leaders of the churches. For the implications of the International Missionary Council, the Faith and Order Conferences and the negotiations for reunion which were completed in South India in 1947 increasingly interested Australian Christian leaders. Many Anglicans believed the Church of South India was unacceptable. They refused to recognise its bishops and ministry, or admit the missionary implications of such reunion. Bishop Batty of Newcastle in 1948 was severely critical about the way in which it allegedly permitted ministers to pick and choose which phrases of the Creed they accepted, thus giving no guarantee of its orthodoxy in faith. He was not able to see that there were similar problems in the Church of England!

Religion and Law

That was brought out in the celebrated Red Book Case between 1944 and 1948. Bishop Wylde of Bathurst, a very typical Anglo-Catholic, was not satisfied with the 1662 Book of Common Prayer and authorised a supplement which was considerably more 'advanced'. A group of church members protested at this imposition, but were completely disregarded. They raised the matter with Mowll, who advised Wylde to withdraw the book. He refused, claiming that as a bishop he had the authority and responsibility for the worship in his diocese. The result was an appeal to the Equity Court of New South Wales by the laity concerned. They were assisted by Minton Taylor, a lawyer with considerable knowledge of ecclesiastical law from his activities in the Sydney and General Synods, and by Principal T. C. Hammond of Moore College. He was an unyielding opponent of Anglo-Catholicism, because he believed it was undermining the historic foundations of Anglicanism. While his motives are not entirely clear, he may have hoped that an adverse decision against Wylde might make it possible to claim that the whole pattern of Anglo-Catholic practice was illegal and at one stroke undermine their power in Australia.

The case provides fascinating evidence for the beliefs of ordinary Anglicans and how helpless they were in the hands of skilled lawyers for Wylde's defence. It also showed that there were serious ambiguities in Wylde's position. The decision of the Court was clear. The Church of England's statutory basis was binding in Australia and the plaintiffs' complaints were substantially upheld. The decision sent shock waves through the Anglican establishment and gave Evangelicals cause for rejoicing. Not surprisingly, Wylde appealed. There was a little comfort in the High Court verdict. The decision of the Equity Court was held to apply only to parishes with particular trusts, something which left Wylde free to use liturgical discretion, but only in part of his diocese. He decided not to appeal to the Privy Council, in consideration of having costs waived.[4]

The intersection of the legal and the spiritual had seldom been more clearly demonstrated. The 1907 Frackleton case in the Presbyterian Church of Queensland had underlined that churches were accountable to the courts for use of their own procedures, which could not deny natural justice. The Red Book case demonstrated that property trusts were a lay defence against episcopal innovation and authoritarianism in worship. Evangelical Anglicans were all the more determined to resist any departure from the authority of law in negotiations about a new constitution for General Synod, even if the Red Book decision showed that they could not get rid of Anglo-Catholic ceremonial and the theology which lay behind it.

Attempts to draft a new constitution had reached a stalemate by 1950 and a despondent Bishop Batty proposed a moratorium on further discussion, after debate in General Synod showed once again that no progress was possible. The positions of Sydney Evangelicals and the Anglo-Catholics were irreconcilable. At that point, Archbishop Fisher of Canterbury, visiting his son in Australia, interposed and suggested that fresh attempts be made, promising a draft from his own hand to get negotiation moving. There was an influential group in Sydney, including Mowll and Hammond who were willing to accept the new proposals. Though they could not persuade the doubters like D. B. Knox of Moore College, or D. W. B. Robinson, (now Archbishop), and some of their laity, the Sydney Synod passed the proposed new constitution, which came into operation in 1962. That gave the Anglican Church a new framework for co-operation nationally. Adelaide also accepted the Constitution, but with the proviso that it could secede under certain circumstances. Anglo-Catholics could be quite as unyielding as Evangelicals, over what they regarded as essentials to unity within the Catholic tradition.[5]

Reunion Again

Congregationalists and Methodists also re-opened negotiations about reunion with Presbyterians after the war ended. The initial proposals for federal union were an attempt to marry theological insights about Christian unity with Australian experience of federation, rather than the creation of an organically united church. Despite the support of many influential Presbyterians, there was too much opposition for the General Assembly of Australia to agree. Once again the other two churches were forced to explore reunion together. That was not easy, because of the disparity of sizes in the two denominations and the ability of the Methodists still to expand with the rapidly rising population, without needing the help of another church. It was not theological convictions or different patterns of polity that held them apart. In 1954 a further invitation was issued to the Presbyterians, which was accepted and the Joint Commission on Church Union was formed in 1957. By 1959, the first Report, *The Faith of the Church* had been issued and was circulated for discussion. That was followed in March, 1963 by another report on *The Church*, plus a proposed *Basis of Union.*

The method followed by the Joint Commission had several sources. There were other schemes for reunion in North America, Britain and the Commonwealth. The convictions of a number of leading ecumenists were reflected in the local decision to seek first unity of faith, then to explore the nature of the church, before dealing with the detail of constitutional and legal matters. The impact of the theology of Barth and Brunner was quite significant, as was Bishop Lesslie Newbigin of South India who spoke at an influential ecumenical conference in Melbourne early in 1960. In Professor J. D. McCaughey of Melbourne the Commission had one who was intimate with British and Genevan ecumenism and whose sharp intelligence was very influential in the discussions and drafting. Other influential members of the Commission were Principal Northey and J. A. Garrett of the Congregational Union, Drs. G. C. Barber and A. H. Wood of the Methodist Church, Professor J. F. Peter and Principal A. Dougan of the Presbyterians. Skilful use was made of younger theologians like Colin Williams, George Yule, Michael Owen, Eric Osborn and Harvey Perkins. A careful balance of state representation was needed, but it was soon clear that the major problems were to come from Presbyterian opponents who saw the scheme as an attempt to move the Presbyterian Church off its historic foundations. No matter what amendments were made and agreed by the other churches, this coalition of opponents were not interested in any compromise which obscured their convictions.[6]

Their obduracy meant that provision had to be made for a continuing Presbyterian church, even though its size was not clear during the 'sixties. There was one path which may have roused wider opposition—the proposal to enter a concordat with the Church of South India, so the union began with the historic episcopate, and close ties with the increasingly important Asian basin. A dissenting reservation in 1963, signed by seven influential Methodists and Presbyterians mortally wounded the proposal and it was fallen from—to the dismay of some Presbyterians who felt the proposals were then not Catholic enough. An attempt to persuade the Anglican Church to join in 1966 was also rejected by the General Synod, for a number of reasons, not least the lateness of the time and the absence of anything like the fundamental declarations of the Anglican Constitution. Also, the studied vagueness of the 1970 revised *Basis of Union* seemed to people like Dr. K. Rayner (now Archbishop of Adelaide) to have serious weaknesses in ministry, doctrinal authority and the sacraments.

One of the most important features of the Commission's work and the details of the *Basis* was the conviction that reunion must be accompanied by careful attention to renewal, so that the proposed church was committed to its missionary task within and beyond Australia. Each of the negotiating Churches had a strong concern that the central convictions of the Reformation must be at the centre of the new church's life. This resulted in a collection of doctrinal statements along the lines proposed by the United Presbyterian Church of the USA, rather than the production of a new confession for the uniting church. All the details of the reunion must, it was argued, be congruous with the Gospel revealed in Jesus Christ. There was a much more ecumenical and theological context to this set of negotiations than those occurring earlier in the century.[7] The quality of the reports produced compared favourably with any of the overseas schemes—an indication of the maturity and vision of the

Australian negotiating churches. Translating that vision of unity, renewal and mission into language understood by local congregations took an enormous amount of energy and time, all the more remarkable when the Joint Commission had no secretariat of its own and people like Professor Yule travelled widely in their own time to explain the issues. All was done on a voluntary basis, by people who already had daunting commitments.

Human frailty, however, crept in. The questions for the first vote in 1972 were confusing for many voters. The Presbyterian votes were very hard to interpret, because there had already been intensive lobbying to ensure that particular congregations voted one way or another. Another vote to clarify the confusion was held and that gave a sufficient majority for the 1974 General Assembly, together with the Congregational Union and Methodist Conference to vote in favour of the scheme. The 1973 proportions in favour were as follows:– Congregational 85%; Methodist 83%; Presbyterian 69%. One group of Presbyterians submitted "A Claim of Right" to the General Assembly, following the precedent of the 1843 Disruption in Scotland, asserting that they were the authentic Presbyterian Church of Australia and forming their own General Assembly. The main group who had decided to continue did not separate until the Uniting Church in Australia was formed on 22 June, 1977.

The rejoicing that, after three quarters of a century, the three churches had united was tempered by grief at leaving familiar buildings, the division of families and friends and the uncertainties about life in a new context. As happens in many reunions, there was a significant fallout of membership over the next decade—an estimated 37,000 by 1980. Opposition to and disillusion with reunion was only one of the reasons for that. Churches which had not united, like the Anglican Church, had a similar decline of commitment, according to a number of the indicators which provide a rough guide—baptisms, attendance at communion, confirmations, marriages. That decline from the peak reached by all the major churches around the year 1960 was not just an Australian phenomenon.[8] All over the English-speaking and European Christian world there was similar decline, with the Roman Catholic Church facing the same cold draughts.

There was one reunion in Australia which attracted less public notice than the formation of the Uniting Church, but it was a remarkable achievement nonetheless. The formation of the Lutheran Church of Australia in 1966 healed divisions that went back to the beginnings of German settlement in South Australia.[9] Lutheran commitment to pure doctrine had resulted in a number of schisms, because of the entanglement of doctrinal and personal disagreements with Lutheran divisions in Germany and North America. There were still separate ethnic Lutheran congregations, related to the churches in their homeland, like the Swedish, German and Finnish groups, but the Lutheran Church covered a range of groups more comprehensive than the Lutheran union completed in 1987 in the United States. This was yet another example of the way the Australian environment has brought together ethnic confessional churches more rapidly than elsewhere. American Methodists did not unite till 1939 and the wounds of civil war kept the two major Presbyterian Churches in the United States apart until 1983.

Orthodox Expansion

The other major group of churches in which ethnicity and unity have proved strongly incompatible are the Orthodox Churches.[10] So far they have largely repeated the ecclesiological patterns of the ethnic churches which preceded them in Australia, for it was not until after 1945 that migration had made them a major component in Australian Christianity. Their presence goes back to 1820 when Father Dionisii of the visiting Russian ship, the "Vostok," held services at Kiribilli Point in Sydney. A Service also appears to have been held on a visiting Russian warship in Port Phillip Bay in 1862. In 1895, Archimandrite Dorotheos held services in Sydney and Melbourne for the small Greek communities and the foundation for Holy Trinity, Surry Hills was laid in May, 1898. At this stage the Greek Patriarchate of Jerusalem took jurisdiction, but in 1903 the Synod of Greece took over and that was approved by the Ecumenical Patriarchate in 1908. Another strand of Orthodoxy entered about 1911 with the arrival of Syrian Orthodox in Sydney. Then on the 7 March, 1924, the Ecumenical Patriarchate established the Metropolis of Australia and New Zealand to have jurisdiction over *all* Orthodox in this region. There was a good deal of tension under the first bishop, Christophoros, and divisions occurred in both Melbourne and Sydney. Timotheos, his successor from 1931–47, was not entirely free of troubles, but he established a framework of law and important foundations in education and social work, before he returned to be Metropolitan of Rhodes. The strength of the Greek Orthodox Communities and their strong lay leaders made life very difficult for Metropolitan Theophylactos between 1947–58, for the pace of migration was increasing rapidly, with an estimated 75,000 in the Orthodox community by 1954. The establishment of other orthodox churches like the Ukrainian (1948) the Serbian (1949) the Bulgarian (1950) the Russian (1958) the Macedonian (1960) the Roumanian (1973) made an exceedingly complex mix incompatible with the 1924 decision. Many of them had splits and bitter conflicts between clergy and laity, because of competing jurisdictions outside Australia and actions by bishops whose canonical status is disputed, as well as frictions over property and personalities, which have been so common in all the Australian churches in their early years. Though canonically there can only be one Orthodox bishop in one place, it is likely to be many decades before such visible unity can be realised. Even creating a common meeting ground in the Standing Conference of the Canonical Orthodox Churches of Australia, founded in 1977 has proved impossible.

Nevertheless, the Greek Orthodox Church, the major group, has grown steadily in unity and maturity.[11] Clergy and laity conferences have been held since 1961 (1965, 1972, 1981, 1985), and Archbishop Stylianos, who was enthroned in 1975, has given judicious leadership, despite the fact that there are still a number of Orthodox congregations which do not recognise him. His theological scholarship and experience in ecumenism has made him an important member of the Australian Council of Churches, along with Bishop Gibran of the Antiochene Orthodox. The number of priests has not kept pace with the growth of population and it has been difficult sometimes to find men willing to come. The foundation of St.Andrew's Theological College in Redfern in 1986, with a very well-qualified staff, has been a very important step in providing future Australian priests and religious with an education which is both local and traditional. Establishing monasteries has proved more difficult, though there are now foundations for both Greek and Serbian jurisdictions. Although many Australians find Orthodoxy somewhat exotic and daunting because of the language and cultural barriers, a beginning has been made with occasional services in English. If American experience is any guide, there will be a gradual growth in converts through marriage and personal choice, which steadily helps these churches to become Australian, without losing their identity as Orthodox. The opening of an Orthodox secondary school in Melbourne in 1987 followed a well-trodden path established by other churches., The language schools which some of the Orthodox and Uniate Churches have established have appealed to a significant group, but not a majority. Since liturgy is not in the vernacular anyway and the ethos of the Orthodox Churches is very different from that of either Protestants or Roman Catholics, that may not be a long-term barrier. For the orthodox the visual is as important as the auditory, and a sense of the mysterious and transcendent has always surpassed rational understanding in their tradition.

The Orthodox have joined the other churches in the pattern of providing clergy, buildings and schools. This has made the post-1945 period a time of building not surpassed since the late 19th century. The succession of suburbs built to house both natural increase and migrants has enormously enlarged all the capital cities and many of the second rank cities. By the 'fifties it was becoming clear that many once flourishing churches were becoming redundant in the inner-city suburbs, as housing patterns changed. Some were purchased by migrants, others were taken over for business or cultural purposes, or simply demolished.

Dealing with Growth

In the new areas, once the initial shortages of building materials were overcome, halls and houses for clergy usually preceded the building of a permanent church. Another generation of old and new Australians learned the cost of providing places of worship, religious education and community service, while they were establishing their own homes and careers. Most denominations provided short-term loans until new congregations reached the point of self-support, or well-established congregations were encouraged to adopt new causes. The financial and administrative strains were heavy and it was not surprising that some began to ask whether there was not a better way, either through new forms of Christian presence or through partnership, of being the Church in new housing areas.[12] That involved both theological analysis and bold experiment in the 'sixties and 'seventies.

Experiments along those lines tended first to occur in struggling inner city suburbs, like Collingwood where ecumenical partnership seemed to offer a very contemporary ministry that could deal with migratory populations. In Victoria, the Rev. G. Bucknall, of the Presbyterian Church, had a compelling vision of new styles of ministry and discipleship, which were partly based on American models and partly on his own shrewd observation of city life in Australia.[13] Some bold experiments occurred as the reunion negotiations gathered momentum, some joint ventures were established in new housing areas and experiments in team ministry begun. At Queen's College, Melbourne, Professor Colin Williams introduced Methodist students to new thought on mission, ministry and church life, before he left for the Divinity School, University of Chicago, to exert a major influence on theological education in the United States. Traditional patterns of worship, preaching and pastoral care all came under sharp questioning by the mid-sixties and many Protestant divinity students saw service in the city as a more attractive option than ministry in the suburbs, portrayed as captive to outdated values and styles of discipleship. Some of the ablest students left ministry within the institutional church altogether, for work in other agencies, or even to test the exciting waters of politics and non-stipendiary ministry. That was not nearly so obvious in Moore and Ridley Colleges where the influence of Principals Knox and Morris kept Anglican students very much more in the Evangelical and Reformed tradition.

The immediate post-war years had promised none of this ferment. Work was re-established very much on traditional lines, though the Anglicans did appoint men like Ted Buckle, (now Bishop in Auckland), to work among the varied communities on the vast Snowy Mountains hydro-electric schemes. There was some sympathy for refugees and migrants from non-British cultures, like the Balts, but most Christians assumed that the migrants would learn English and adapt to existing lifestyles. The emphasis of governments was on British migration to begin with, for patriotism was still strong. Archbishop Moline's sermons in Perth's Anglican Cathedral on the accession and visit of Queen Elizabeth 11 underlined that.[14]

Only as it became clear that such sources were not able to meet government targets did the net spread to Italy, Greece, Yugoslavia, Germany, Holland and Central Europe. Some attempt was made to bring priests and ministers from migrant homelands and the Presbyterians gained some fine Dutch ministers like Professor H. Spykerboer in Queensland and the Rev. Marius Geursen in Victoria, as well as a cluster of talented new Scots and Irish imports like Professors John McIntyre, Haultain Brown and Crawford Millar of Sydney and Davis McCaughey in Melbourne (now Governor of Victoria), who was in particular to make such a notable contribution to his adopted homeland. The basic assumption was that migrants would be assimilated rapidly, but the Dutch soon showed otherwise. A number found the Presbyterian Church of Australia far too liberal and they founded the Reformed Churches of Australia in 1951 and an alternative theological college at Geelong in 1955 which they hoped would grow into a Christian University like the Free University of Amsterdam.

Some Roman Catholic migrants found the Irish Catholicism of Australia very puritanical and restrictive, with none of the colour to which they were used, or such an open relation to the cultural life of the nation.[15] Parishes were often slow to recognise the need for special services and facilities to help their co-religionists to feel at home. The churches of migrants were also slow to send clergy and chaplains to Australia, for they were pre-occupied with postwar reconstruction. Despite the fact that Australia mainly was a nation of migrants and descendants of migrants, few of British and Irish stock remembered their struggle to adapt to Australia, and expected the new arrivals to learn the hard way, as they had. Many did just that, but it was tragic that the churches were able to do so little to modify the suspicion and hostility with which so many migrants were greeted when they queried Australian *mores*. The Catholic Immigration Offices and the Resettlement Committee of the Australian Council of Churches did splendid work with limited resources and shoestring facilities.[16] Many clergy who acted as chaplains on migrant ships, or who met ships, did noble pastoral work with bewildered new arrivals. On a population basis, Australia took as high a percentage of refugees as any other nation, for which her Churches can take much credit.

The British migrants were mostly from the cities where the impact of the established churches was weakest, so that they did not contribute much to a rise in the active membership of the churches to which they had nominal allegiance. Among clergy however it was a different story. The Anglican episcopate was enriched by a number of notable arrivals like Archbishops Halse, Gough, Grindrod, Arnott, Moline, Appleton, Woods and Penman, who deepened and strengthened the Anglican sense of belonging to a world-wide communion, Theologians like Hebert and Snell went to Adelaide. In Melbourne, the sense of Britishness was kept alive by Sir Irving Benson of Wesley Central Mission until his retirement in 1967. Among Congregationalists, Drs. Raymond Abba and Harold Leatherland reminded their co-religionists that some aspects of Australian Congregationalism were far removed from their ancient heritage. Principal Mervyn Himbury did the same among Victorian Baptists, until he retired from Whitley College in 1986. European migrants have yet to make the same contribution to church leadership that they have made to industry, business and the professions, though the Lutherans' Professor Hermann Sasse was influential.

Some migrants found one aspect of Australia familiar. There was a significant influence of the Communist Party in the trade unions, journalism and education, as well as in the civil service and in various front cultural organisations. For those refugees who had known the repression of Communism at first hand many Australians seemed astonishingly innocent and complacent about the threat they were harbouring. The 1951 referendum on the suppression of the Communist Party showed a divided Australia. The growing impact of the cold war affected some in Australian churches, especially the small idealistic minority like the Revs. F. Coaldrake, (briefly Archbishop elect of Brisbane's Anglicans), J.E. Owen, A. Dickie and F. Hartley, Melbournians who were concerned about world peace, attended peace conferences, and did not wish to place the human race exclusively into Communist and Anti-Communist camps, with freedom found only on the western side of the Iron Curtain.[17] They had sharp opposition, and Dickie's North Essendon Presbyterian congregation even tried to starve him out. The visit of Dr. Hromadka of Prague to Australia in 1954 showed how bitterly some migrants resented church sponsorship of his visit. They saw him as a traitor not a mediator.

The crippling strikes of the late 'forties were overcome partly by the resolution of governments, but even more by the steady battle Santamaria's union allies conducted against Communist influence in unions.[18] According to received wisdom, the British and European working classes were largely alienated from the churches, apart from pious pockets like Wales. The significance of the influence of Roman Catholic laity in the Australian union movement was an indication that the thesis of such secularisation needs some modification. Sections of the Liberal and Country parties were strongly anti-communist, but they had very different class interests and bases, and were incapable of influencing the union movement from within.

Changing Boundaries

The leadership of Mr. Robert G. Menzies while Prime Minister was a fascinating symbol of Protestant values and a profound suspicion of socialism and communism. He had risen from humble origins, been educated at Wesley College and the University of Melbourne. His activities in the Presbyterian Bible Class movement were long remembered and though he did not parade his faith, it should not be forgotten, despite its scant mention in his autobiography. Many Presbyterians were almost deliberately committed to keeping their inner beliefs away from prying eyes. Superficially that could be interpreted as a sign of conformity to increasingly secular attitudes in the Australian community, but in many cases it rested on deep convictions about the importance of keeping the sacred and the secular apart. One of Menzies' addresses most remembered was on "Christianity and the secular", but unfortunately it does not appear to have survived in his papers. His patriotism and exuberant admiration for the Crown did not make him any less Australian than his Labor opponents. He stood for a different constellation of values and his passion for educational opportunity is one of the most obvious features of his Protestantism, providing his most enduring legacy.[19]

By the end of the sixties, it was clear that the social role of the Protestant churches and their influence had changed. The laws relating to gambling had steadily relaxed and widened opportunities, not only in the racing industry, but also in the clubs which were so widely patronised in New South Wales. The defeat of their campaign against the South Australian government's proposal in 1965 to liberalise gambling was a reminder to the Methodist Church there that its attitudes were no longer in line with those of many of its own members. Support for Sunday observance by legal penalties was steadily diminished, opening up possibilities for sport, entertainment and consumption of alcohol, which a previous generation would have found shocking. Few in the churches believed any more that sabbath observance in the old style was essential to the nation's spiritual and moral well-being. It was simply a matter of individual conscience. The same progress can be seen in the liquor laws, especially in the end of six o'clock closing which disappeared in Victoria in 1966.[20] The latter case is of special interest to the historian, for the Rev. John Westermann, the head of the Christian Citizenship Department was a key person in persuading the Methodist Conference that the end of this particular law would be of social benefit.

For Roman Catholics, the litmus test of personal obedience to the teaching of the church was the use of contraception. Despite the teaching of *Humanae vitae* on birth control, a number of priests and laity publicly opposed papal teaching, because it appeared to have gone against the evidence submitted to the drafters of the encyclical. In the years following 1968, it became clear that a number of priests were advising those who confessed to the sin of using contraceptive devices that it was a matter for individual conscience. For many Catholics this decision was the end of their unquestioning acceptance of papal infallibility. Even though they continued in all other respects to be loyal to their church, they too placed more weight on personal choice and responsibility.[21]

Since 1962 the impact of the Second Vatican Council on all the major Australian churches has been enormous. It pulled down the walls between the Roman Catholic Church and other bodies and made ecumenism a virtue and not a vice. The contrast between the old views of Christian unity and the new can be vividly seen in the pamphlet *Christian Unity in God's Way*, published in 1951. The Rev. J. A. Conellan said that:

> Catholics believe that there can be no question at all of reunion of churches. The real church of Christ has never been divided... Unity can only be secured in one way—God's way—by entrance into that Society, the Catholic Church, which God himself set up to bring men into union with Him.[22]

The advice of the Vatican Council's Decree on Ecumenism (1964) is quite different, recognising as it does the reality of other churches and what the Decree on the Church describes as "ecclesial communities". The importance of all Christians entering more deeply into their common heritage was recognised, if faith was to be authentically Catholic, for some recognition was given to the ways in which all churches have obscured divine truth. The divisive impact of mixed marriages, which could poison family relations for a lifetime, was modified by abolition of the requirement that the non-Catholic partner must sign an undertaking that the children be brought up as Roman Catholics. That was now only required of the Catholic partner. Dispensations can be granted for marriages to take place in other churches, or with clergy of other denominations taking part. There are no longer the prohibitions against entering another Church's building for a wedding, or the humiliating vestry weddings. In 1964 the Mass in English was initiated.

Protestants and Catholics have joined in study circles, in Palm Sunday Peace Marches and ecumenical services, in acts of social service and in the publication of ecumenical documents on social justice. The old employment barriers have almost disappeared and care agencies or schools run by the churches mostly employ staff on a professional rather than a confessional basis. Religious still tend to hold the position of principal in Catholic secondary schools, even though a huge majority of the teachers are now lay. That in turn has been the consequence of state aid to Church schools resuming after almost a century in the eastern states. Though Catholic agitation for rectification of this injustice continued, the major parties were not disposed to reopen the question and the Protestant Churches were still adamantly opposed, as late as the 1950s, to public money being used to teach Romish error.[23]

The initial breakthrough came with the Federal government in 1956 offering loans to churches to encourage them to build secondary schools in Canberra, to make the move of civil servants from Melbourne and Sydney more attractive. By 1960, the political consequences of the Split in the Labor Party and the formation of the Democratic Labor Party gave Mr. Menzies the opportunity to exploit Labor disarray and further split the Roman Catholic vote. His offer of federal aid was initially rejected by Protestant Churches, but their school boards and councils saw the possibility of taking pressure off fees. By the mid-sixties that wall between Protestants and Catholics had fallen, because state governments had also seen the political advantages of giving aid on a *per capita* basis. The years since have seen steady increases of aid, which have given burgeoning Catholic schools something equal to state and independent schools' facilities and teacher/pupil ratios. Even more important, it has removed one of the deep senses of grievance which kept the Catholic community from fully identifying with a State which they believed was still inflicting protestant style discrimination on them. The way was opened for more Catholics to enter the Liberal and Country Parties and then to be selected for state and federal parliaments from those traditionally Protestant parties. The professional advantages from state aid to Catholic teachers have been enormous, and the development of far greater lay participation in the control of schools has been of more importance in breaking down artificial barriers between laity, religious or clergy than many of the decrees of Vatican II.

Personal relationships were also important in the breakdown of old sectarian stereotypes. The friendship of Archbishops Duhig and Halse in Brisbane was widely noted by their people. Archbishop Frank Woods' Christmas call on Archbishop Mannix in 1958 was similarly influential. In Sydney, the refusal of the Anglican Archbishops of Sydney to be associated with Papal welcomes has not prevented close personal relations of an informal kind. In Melbourne, the friendship of Father Percy Jones and the McCaugheys began at Ormond College, when they met privately with the Anglican Father G. Hebert in 1953 who, despondent about ecumenicism in South Australia, came to Melbourne to see if Victoria would be more open. Mannix gave permission for Father Jones and Cleary to continue meeting with a small group of Presbyterians and Anglicans. One result was the 1955 Week of Prayer of Christian Unity. This group also took soundings on state aid, for it was clear that the attitude of Presbyterians and Anglicans in Victoria would be politically vital to Menzies' government.[24]

By 1973, there was an ecumenical service in the Eucharistic Congress that year in Melbourne. Even more significant in the long term was the association of some leading Catholic liturgists as advisers to those working on the production of a new Prayer Book for the Anglican Church. There was also significant cross fertilisation in the Communion Services produced for the Uniting Church. There is now mutual recognition of baptism and a common baptismal certificate, and a widely-shared lectionary. *The Australian Hymn Book* (1977), with its Catholic Supplement has been one of the most successful recent hymnals, with an international sale.

Such co-operation is not simply the recognition of shared weakness in the face of a more secular society. Its roots lay deep in the Christian tradition, even if they were overlaid by the hatreds engendered by the Reformation and its aftermath. The bi-lateral dialogues through which the Australian churches have moved into deeper understanding of each other were initially opened up between 1967–80 by the Australian Council of Churches on sensitive subjects like the Eucharist. The international confessional dialogues, involving a number of Australians, have also done an enormous amount to remove misunderstandings and identify the real differences between the major Christian families. The Australian dialogues do not have the massive theological expertise that some of the international and North American dialogues have called on, but they have made very real progress nevertheless, exploring sensitive issues relating to ministry, authority and sacraments. Australians are finding that their catholic heritage is richer and more widely shared than they dreamed.

The development of ecumenical theological education has been another achievement with major implications for the future. There had been limited co-operation in Melbourne between Baptists, Congregationalists and Methodists at the beginning of the century, with some input from the Presbyterians, but there was nothing formalised and enduring. In Sydney, Congregationalists and Presbyterians co-operated from the beginning of the century and were joined by Methodists in 1926 until unease at the views of Professor Angus led to their withdrawal from his classes. The establishment of the Faculty of Divinity at Sydney University and the recognition of Church teachers made it possible for Anglicans to work with other Protestants even though the colleges stayed very separate. That is still the deliberate choice of Moore College, even though it works within the framework of the Australian College of Theology.[25]

In Melbourne, a different partnership developed in 1963 because of the physical closeness of Methodist and Presbyterian theological institutions. They were joined by the Anglicans of Trinity College and the Congregational College at Kew, in 1969 to form the United Faculty of Theology. The major change came with the decision of the Jesuits to move their theologate from Pymble in 1969 to Parkville and join the United Faculty of Theology in 1972. That would have not been possible without Vatican II, nor without the personal relationships between leading Jesuits and the Master of Ormond College, Dr. Davis McCaughey which led to agreements about the amalgamation of the Jesuit, Methodist and Presbyterian libraries to form the finest theological collection in Australia. The United Faculty of Theology which resulted is unique in our country and a source of amazement to overseas visitors, because of the substantial integration of teaching and government, without the pastoral formation of the partners' students being removed from its distinctive setting in their own ecclesial tradition. Roman Catholic entry into the Melbourne College of Divinity in 1972 followed by the Churches of Christ, has provided a still wider context for partnership in theological education and postgraduate study.

Another ecumenism which has had significant public impact, has been through the evangelistic crusades of Billy Graham and his team since 1959. Though the long term impact of these has been difficult to assess objectively, their symbolic importance was immense. They were a Protestant equivalent of the great Catholic Eucharistic Congresses, making visible a unity of faith and action, that led to the deepening of personal faith and the commitment of many to new kinds of service. Their music, drama and the atmosphere generated by such huge crowds gave Graham's message an impact which was unusual. The number of new members in many of the participating churches peaked after the campaign, as did the numbers offering as candidates for ministry and missionary service. The impact of the Methodist Mission to the Nation in 1952 and the evangelism of many other Churches were also tributaries which fed the river and brought the spiritual searching of many to a satisfying focus.[26]

Critics were not silenced, but Graham's visits undoubtedly gave mass evangelism a new appeal, the more so as he modestly disclaimed any desire to build a new denomination. He also underlined the continuing importance and lasting effectiveness of parish evangelism. His visit was a reminder to the churches in the Australian Council of Churches that there were other patterns of ecumenism, which appealed to those distrustful of organic and organisational unity. This "spiritual" unity for evangelism and mission, was very important to Evangelicals, many of whom were suspicious about the ecumenisms of Geneva and Rome, because of their allegedly political content. Sydney Anglicans were more successful than most in keeping relations with different ecumenisms, and at reminding their Anglo-Catholic brethren that reunion with Rome and Constantinople was not the only important item on the ecumenical agenda.

Though sectarianism has not disappeared from Australia, the ecumenism of the last twenty-five years has done much to modify stereotypes and lead to all kinds of new networks and coalitions within and between churches, which have given a new meaning to the word "catholic". The emergence of significant Pentecostal Churches and the survival of Evangelicalism, despite liberal prophecies of its disappearance make the development of unity with these varieties of Protestantism, as well as with the Orthodox, an important contribution to the development of Australian Christianity. In a very real way the tolerance that has co-existed with sectarian nastiness, has been one of the foundations on which to build a nation in which there are now not only many Christian variations, but also representatives of most of the great religions. Christians have discovered that their common faith and humanity transcends ethnic and religious differences. They now have the responsibility to bear witness that such unity is possible between a new mix of cultures and religions, without diminishing the integrity of their catholic heritage.

CHAPTER FIVE:

The Future of our Past

Since the 1960s, there has been a marked increase in the variety of Australian religiosity, ranging from small migrant groups from historic churches like the Assyrians and the Copts to exotic sects from Asia and North America, of whom the Moonies and the International Society for Krishna Consciousness are the most widely known. There are a variety of groups related in different ways to the schools of Hinduism and Buddhism, as well as the divisions of Islam and Judaism.[1] In addition, there have been many groups established which follow therapists and gurus of varying significance. For example, the followers of Mrs. Anne Hamilton-Byrne in Victoria, appear to have regarded her as a 'Christ' figure, whose commands justified the manipulation of adopted children. The desire to experience new kinds of community, led a number of thoughtful and idealistic people to reject the patterns of vocation, family life and religion with which they had grown up. Their attempt to establish new patterns of social bonding in uncontaminated rural retreats can be seen as a secular monasticism, but they often discovered that to abolish the boundaries of authority, family and property created a whole series of problems which they did not have the spiritual and personal resources to solve.

Some of these communities have been intentionally Christian. Those with Baptist origins, like the Brisbane House of Freedom and the House of the Gentle Bunyip (1975) in Melbourne were ecumenical and involved a core group who were vowed to a simple rule of life and sharing of goods. That enabled them to undertake a wide range of imaginative community service and caring. Though evangelical in their theology, their high degree of social involvement was very disturbing to many who valued traditional boundaries. The Bunyips were regarded with suspicion by some of their fellow Baptists. At their best, such groups have opened up new horizons of discipleship, but they have often learned some hard lessons about the intractable sinfulness and selfishness of partly-redeemed human nature.[2]

Other Christians, influenced by the New Testament models of the house church, have moved away from the historic churches to create small and intimate fellowships, where the gifts of the whole body of believers could be exercised. While this movement has not developed the momentum of the British house church networks, it has had some very strong leadership and the capacity to learn, because of the influence of people like Dr. Robert Banks, a former Anglican academic, who has become a para-church leader of national and international stature. John Smith of Melbourne from a Methodist family, has been another very significant pioneer, with his notoriety as an evangelist to the bikies and social dropouts through God's Squad. His Truth and Liberation Concern was a fascinating example of a church which grew out of compassion for the broken. Smith has since founded Care and Communication Concern based at St. Martin's Community Church since 1984. Whether such groups will become indigenous churches in their own right, growing through the crisis of losing their first generation leadership remains to be seen. But they give the lie to the claim that Australian Christians have not produced any homegrown churches. Older organisations, like Scripture Union, adapted imaginatively to new opportunities to work with youth.[3]

Era of the Spirit

Among Pentecostals, some of this creative separatism has been inspired by the imitation of American and South Korean models and sometimes by personal rivalries. It has led to a number of large congregations in the last two decades, which have few parallels in the historic churches, like that of Frank Houston in downtown Sydney, or of Pastor R. Kliminiok at Mt. Gravatt. Some in this tradition are planning for mega-churches with several thousand members and a bewildering variety of networks and activities, including a new type of Christian school.

Rapid growth of pentecostal-type churches has been one of the most unexpected features of the religious scene since the watershed of the sixties, and the development of a counter-culture which seemed, at a number of points, very opposed to traditional Christianity. They have been uncompromising in their opposition to liberal Christianity, claiming to draw their guidance from the Bible alone and seeking to recreate first century Christianity down to every organisational detail. Interest in traditional eschatology, demonology and an active involvement in spiritual healing have been most recently accompanied by an emphasis that authentic Christianity must be accompanied by signs and wonders. The large following that John Wimber, the American prophet of this approach, has already attracted since his 1987 Canberra conference is an indication that the currents of conservative religion are running rather more strongly than the leaders of the historic churches have estimated.[4]

In part that is a reflection of trends in other parts of the world, especially in Britain and the United States, where the pattern of partnership and accommodation with the perceivedly relevant segments of culture has caused a significant decline in membership in major churches with a liberal tradition. Unashamedly conservative churches like the Southern Baptists, have continued to grow against the trends, both by conversion and transfer of religious consumers who have found their previous sources of religious affiliation unsatisfactory. While there is not yet a thorough survey of pentecostal church growth in Australia, which would give an accurate picture of how much is by evangelism of the unchurched and how much attraction of the dissatisfied from other churches, there is some evidence that the latter predominate. Nor is there any strong evidence that the pentecostal churches in Australia have focussed the religious aspirations of the marginal and the dispossessed, whereas their counterparts in the United States and Latin America have had precisely such a role.

Within the major churches, the influence of the charismatic type of renewal has been important in the evangelical groups who have felt excluded from leadership since the 1920s. In many cases there has been a simple move from evangelical enthusiasm to speaking in tongues, and involvement in healing and prayer meetings, which have a striking affinity with the emotional warmth of 19th century Primitive Methodists and Bible Christians. The claim to experience God's presence personally has always been a powerful attraction within the Evangelical tradition in Australia and elsewhere. The weaknesses of exclusive reliance on such conversion led in many congregations to an emphasis on nurture and gradual growth in Christian understanding. There was little place for the drama of spiritual pilgrimage to be celebrated publicly and many people had religious experience which they could not name and were too shy to share. Charismatic piety has reawakened the conversionist tradition and broken through formerly Protestant boundaries into the Roman Catholic community.

That so many from the sixties on, were prepared to experiment with the chemical expansion of consciousness that could occur with the use of LSD, marijuana and heroin, indicated a hunger for spiritual reality which was not satisfied by the liturgies of the major churches. An even more important development of that search during the last twenty years has been the discovery by many Protestants that there are depths of insight about spirituality in Roman Catholic religious orders. That has given new life to their own experience and a fresh valuation of their own religious tradition.

For a period of a decade or more in the sixties, there was a widespread conviction that structures and order were an impossible limitation of the Spirit. Some clergy took a perverse delight in demonstrating their capacity for iconoclasm, whether they were Protestant or Catholic. Dean Hazlewood of Perth, who made some careless remarks about a schizoid Jesus backtracked when rebuked by the Catholic Archbishop. The well-formed convictions of historic Christianity seemed for a whole generation to have lost their power and appeal. New models of education, worship, parish renewal, ministry and evangelism, appeared in bewildering variety. Classical liturgy fostered by Methodists like Austin James was replaced by extempore prayers and happenings, with choruses reflecting the musical taste of pop culture and country and western music.

Theological education for both Protestants and Catholics changed dramatically in content and in style, with students demanding and being given a voice in government of their colleges. A whole generation of students were anxious to experience new styles of ministry and break away from the tyranny of church organisation into what seemed a more open world outside. Many found the demands of unstructured freedom more than they could cope with, especially when congregations unwilling to change showed little enthusiasm to fund brave new ventures. In part that was a failure of vision and courage and a retreat back into the safety of the familiar. It was also a lay protest against clerical modernity, which ignored the spiritual needs of those who cherished the past, because of the enthusiasm with which some clergy surfed along the waves of the future.[5]

Protestants in particular, found it very difficult to cope with these crosscurrents. At some points these changes had close links with cherished Protestant values, such as liberty of conscience, the priority of spirit over structure and the need for continuous reformation. Yet it speedily became apparent that unless denominations kept their historic roots, change for the sake of change could be a very destructive agent of secularisation, which simply accommodated Christianity to contemporary culture. Speaking prophetically about political issues like foreign policy could easily become a dressed-up version of the views of secular analysts, rather than a genuinely critical perspective, which sprang out of costly engagement with both historic revelation and contemporary cultures. It was not surprising that a proportion of clergy educated in the sixties and seventies dropped out of ministry altogether because the Churches were reluctant to change. Some became very successful in business, professions and politics, others disappeared from the institutional churches into the counter-culture.

The Roman Catholic church often dealt sharply with those who were deemed to have moved past the line of obedience to authority. Father Edmund Campion, parish priest of Woolloomooloo, however, managed not only to be a social activist, but also kept enough of the confidence of the hierarchy not to be moved into insignificance. Resignations were more difficult to handle. There were heavy losses of priests and religious, some of whom married, and a dramatic drop in vocations which in turn forced all sorts of changes in Catholic schools and parish staffing.[6] Anglicans, Methodists and Presbyterians experienced a similar fall-off, though the reasons may have been different. Uniting Church candidates for the Synod of Victoria in 1988 are still below the peak numbers of Presbyterian ordinands in the early 'sixties.

Women's Roles

The other dramatic change of the 'sixties and seventies was the final admission of women to the ordained ministry of the Presbyterian and Methodist churches, a little before similar decisions were taken by parent bodies in Britain. That has been a tacit recognition of the widened role of women in society generally and the limiting nature of traditional roles of domesticity. Religious bodies are often among the last to change, though Congregationalists had ordained the Rev. Winifred Kiek in 1927 in Adelaide, long after similar steps had been taken in the same tradition in the United States. Yet the role of women has been a source of deep division in Christian communities. Catholics, Orthodox and some Protestants have been unyielding in their conviction that priesthood and ministry is properly male. They argue that Jesus, the giver of ministry, is male and that Scripture and tradition are virtually unanimous in their endorsement of male headship. While there has been some Christian recognition that the role of women is not only familial and nurturing, advocates of the feminist movement, like Germaine Greer, have sharply challenged the manner in which the churches have contributed to the oppression of women and denial of their gifts outside traditional roles.

That has raised acutely the issue of biblical and historical interpretation, especially within the Anglican Church, which has been deeply divided over the decision of some dioceses to ordain women to the diaconate and the commitment of Archbishop Penman of Melbourne to proceed to ordain women to the priesthood in 1990. The decision of the Apellate Tribunal in 1991 will be awaited with keen interest, both within and beyond the Anglican Church. There has been no resolution yet of disagreement over the revelatory character of the passages which speak of women's subordination in church office. Supporters of women's ordination argue that such passages reflect the culture of the day. That must be sensitively separated from the underlying commitment of the New Testament to a church in which the boundaries between men and women were as finally abolished as the distinction between slave and free. Opponents insist that it is impossible to cut apart revelation and culture in such a manner, without distorting the historic character of Christian religion, by conforming it to the spirit of the present age.[7]

Some of those arguments sound rather similar to the arguments used earlier to deny women entrance to politics and the professions, but they focus the dilemma of churches which have a historic heritage. How is that to be proclaimed in a period of cultural relativism and ferment, without retreating into unyielding conservatism that is unable to hear and answer the questions of its own time? Those who have chosen to ordain women have opted for an interpretation which underlines continued re-appropriation of the faith by a community which is open to its world, but not its cultural prisoner.

That cultural captivity is reflected in these lectures. The history of the churches in Australia has been largely male-dominated. The faithfulness of the work and worship of women in all traditions has gone largely unrecorded because they have, until very recent times, been actively denied leadership roles in both clerical and lay spheres. All the Christian churches have relied to a large extent on the contribution of their female members; their absence from the official records is telling. Recent historical writing has begun to redress that imbalance.

The strength and weakness of the Protestant tradition in Australia is its recognition that every human version of the Gospel can become Law within a generation. Protestants have attempted to bear witness that only Christ is sufficient for salvation. They have common loyalties which place great stress on personal responsibility to God and seek to work out that confession in daily vocation. Resistance to Rome has often appeared to be the centre of Protestantism, but at its best this tradition has sought to bear witness to the universal character of the Gospel and in that sense confessed its authentic Catholicity. It has developed its own institutions, patterns of thought and worship, styles of discipleship and methods of mission and evangelism, always reminding its members of the provisional nature of their faith and good works. There are more than accidental similarities to the discipline and ethos of some of the great religious orders. In its conviction that the beauty of holiness is for the whole people of God, Australian Protestantism has set standards which many Australians have regarded as unreasonable and wowserish. The watershed of the 'sixties has forced them, with other Christians to think again about the future of their past. Has too much weight been placed on individual conscience as a guide and too little on the place of law and custom as guides for many of the decisions of everyday life? Our tradition of a mere two hundred years may provide confusing answers, but the vision of Christian Australia has been a vital part of Protestantism.[8]

Dr. Colin Williams now in the United States at the Aspen Institute, has suggested that Australia is the most secular nation on earth. It is a modern version of Dr. Denney's comment. There are a cluster of meanings around the word "secular", some of which can be hostile to Christianity, some neutral and some friendly. Some features of Australian secularity have deeply Christian roots. We need not be mesmerised into thinking that secularism is a total enemy of the Gospel.[9] The religious neutrality of some of the most important institutions in our society has been a guarantee of religious freedom. The religious tests which Dissenters and Catholics alike rejected as an essential qualification for political office and entry to the civil service and the professions need not be mourned. It has taken longer to grow out of the ethnic and religious tribalism which restricted jobs to holders of particular religious views.

Current equal opportunity legislation directed at discrimination may be very testing for the churches as they seek to safeguard the special character of their institutions as bearers of Christian witness. The Lifeline counselling service in Sydney was, at one stage in the seventies, threatened by a group which felt it would be much more effective if it became a secular counselling agency and dropped any religious requirements from its workers.[10] Church schools have faced serious problems with staff who have rejected aspects of the moral teaching which churches have regarded as essential to Christian family life. The dismissal of the Principal of the Glennie School in Queensland and her appeal in 1988, is an example of that dilemma.

The hospitals, the schools, the university colleges, the care agencies, the savings banks, insurance companies and friendly societies which were founded by Christians seeking to serve their neighbour in Christ's name have sometimes grown away from their founders' aims. Increased size, more professional management, the requirements of the state regulatory agencies and the claims of trade unions have inevitably meant that they have developed a life of their own which is the feature of all large organisations.

It has always been the contention of Protestants, as well as many Catholics, that Christian influence in public and private institutions is seen not only in overt commitment to worship and in symbolic Christian leadership. Equally important is the integrity with which institutions are run, the quality of their staff relations, the nature of their service. It may be an elementary point to insist that there is a distinction between the temporal kingdom and the spiritual kingdom, but Jesus' distinction between what belongs to God and Caesar has not always been observed in communities where the roles of Church and State have not been distinguished with sufficient clarity.

There have been heavy costs in the Australian rejection of established churches, which has impoverished the public domain and needlessly privatised religious commitment. That can be clearly seen in some of the secular humanists who wish to reduce religion to a private conviction without influence on social ethics. The extent to which the teachings of the churches on sexuality and family law have been modified in the last thirty years is startling, indicating a fundamental shift in perceptions both in and outside the churches. There are powerful secularising forces in Australian society which are socially destructive and fearfully costly to the taxpayers, because of the way that they exalt private choice without reference to social responsibility.

Protestants must take some responsibility for that, for it represents part of their teaching, with the transcendent removed and the community ignored. Such secularised protestantism can also be seen in elements of the political left and right who have inherited the conviction that exposure of evils and denunciation of transgressors will bring healing. They have forgotten that there was another part of that prophetic passion which summoned people to remember their own sin and seek a common healing. The Catholic social critic, Ronald Conway, has exposed the limitations of these Australian attitudes.[11]

Historical Prespectives

Christians cannot afford to let others define their history for them, because historical memory is crucial for identity. The history of Australian Christianity is more than a footnote to the story of the formative events in the Roman Empire, Europe and North America which have so significantly shaped our Christian communities. There has been a significantly lay character which has modified the clericalism of parent churches and enabled us to do more justice to the ministry of the whole people of God. There has been a freedom to adapt overseas models to suit Australian conditions, which has given Australian Christianity a rather practical character, often uninterested in the spiritual and intellectual depth of some of our forgotten forebears.

The very size of this continent and fierce state rivalries have worked against the emergence of national leaders even within denominations. We are all products of migrant churches, who have struggled to create their vision of a Christian Australia and to build institutions which embodied that vision. Migrant churches commonly are nostalgic, conservative, deferential to the leaders of their parent bodies and not often inclined to value the qualities of originality and creativity in their leadership. Their very strength has lain in the success with which they bridged the gap between the old world and the new. The example of the North American churches suggests that two centuries is not an unusually long time for migrant churches to take on a life of their own and to make a distinctive contribution to theological scholarship, liturgy, mission and spirituality.

Despite the tragic beginning of our nation, those bitter origins have been transformed by free settlement, opportunity for new life and the adaptation of British institutions. The Churches played a significant part in the change from a colony of lawless subjects and corrupt rulers to a nation where integrity in public life has been the rule rather than the exception. The Christian conviction that voluntary service is honourable has greatly enriched the life of local communities and the nation. As Christians begin their third century in this continent, they face a new kind of lawlessness and corruption which has grown out of our forebears' success in using the riches of this land. The churches may well have a major contribution to make to redeeming that, just as they did with our beginnings. But there is much to learn from our forebears about the qualities of spirit needed to deal with the kind of corruption exposed in Queensland, or in segments of the business and industrial sector, where contempt for morality and law has brought ruin to many.

The protestant work ethic is not enough, in its secularised form, to cope with the injustices of structural unemployment and systemic poverty. Yet a community which forgets the dignity given by honest work, done for the glory of God and the service of neighbour, will run into serious problems. Australians know something about the creation of a society which releases energies and creativity, in ways that the old world would not have thought possible, when it dismissed many migrants as failures.

Christians also know something about being the conscience of the community. That conscience has not always been heeded. Sometimes it was misguided. Australia would be the poorer without Mary McKillop and her dream of educating the children of the poor, Bishop Willson with his pleas for compassion for the convict and the insane, Dr. Duguid in his advocacy of the aborigines, or Archbishop Loane of Sydney and his witness for the poor. If we know our history, we will learn something of the cost of that witness and the divine resources which sustained it against bitter resistance and shortsighted refusal to change.

The Christian future may be more limited than influence on the past suggests. We live in a much more complex society, where change is often slower than in smaller communities, without such inbuilt resistances. Our history suggests that individuals and groups do much to change perceptions and policy. The models provided by Protestant societies and Catholic religious orders may prove very important if our past is to have a creative future. Many opinion makers in our society are very dismissive of Australia's Christian past and have an incredible faith in education to provide what was once expected of churches. They may be convinced that modern industrial societies are held together by the beliefs and practices of modernity rather than religious faith, but the history of attempts to build such societies does not give much cause for confidence.

Australians who know their heritage would want to point out the importance of Christian faith for nation-building.

The splendid Bicentennial history, *Australians* has an ambivalent attitude to religion. The social importance of the Churches is recognised in an unsystematic way and the private beliefs of diarists are noted with interest and sensitivity. But the reader would have to be forgiven who came to the conclusion that religion was basically marginal to the movements which shaped Australian history. Even if it is difficult to explore the connections between belief and behaviour, a great deal of work remains to be done to elucidate that link in government, the public service, the professions, industry, business, grazing and agriculture, as well as in the leadership of the churches themselves. Liberalism and Protestantism were powerful allies in the creation of Australia, though not the only creators. Protestants were committed to modernisation and progress, without always paying attention to the price future generations might have to pay. Nor did they pay sufficient attention to the classical spiritual and theological heritage which made their achievement possible. It is a challenge to Christians in a much more ecumenical society to recover the universality of the Christian heritage for the 21st century.

Patrick O'Farrell, without doubt Australia's most perceptive historian of the relations of religion and society, gave a fascinating paper in 1981 on "The cultural ambivalence of Australian religion". He noted the tension between the marginality of religion in Australia and the remarkable influence of Mr. Santamaria and the Movement, which suggested that there were factors that the thesis of secularisation and marginality simply did not explain.

The development of Evangelical Protestantism is another. Despite its cultural and religious deficiencies, it provided a framework of meaning with which many very ordinary people were comfortable. Diaries and letters, like those of the Presbyterian McIntyres of New England, speak about the impact of illness, natural disasters, financial success and failure, and the realities of death in the context of Providence. The hearing and reading of the Bible, worship and personal prayer opened windows for them, to a transcendent realm.[12] Such evangelical Christian doctrine and ethics gave many Australians a far wider purpose than the daily struggle to survive, however important that was.

Such evidence may not be 'religion' in the fullest cultural sense of European societies, which O'Farrell appears to use as his yardstick. He deplores Australian bigotry, prejudice and sectarianism without mentioning that they were equally obtrusive and destructive in Britain and Europe, despite the presence of what might be termed "high" religious culture and a sense of heritage impossible here. Nor does he do justice to the ways in which many Protestants made important contributions to the debunking of establishment arrogance. Such iconoclasm was not simply anti-clerical. It also offered ways in which ordinary people could grow into responsibility assumed by ministers as of right in Britain. There may be strong materialist overtones to the self-improvement offered by Protestantism, but it gave to many Australians opportunities that were denied to their relatives who stayed in the far more repressive and authoritarian homelands.

Despite the ugliness of sectarian bigotry and violence, Australia never knew the terrible religious hatreds released in the Irish civil wars, or the mutual massacres of Serbs and Croats. Religion may have had a much more domestic and personal role in Australia, but it was rarely tyrannical, despite the strands of puritanism which have evoked such denunciation in *The Bulletin* and *Truth*, or later in the more sophisticated pages of historians tinged with Marxism.

Indeed, one of the reasons why Australian Christians have a slighter sense of history, than some other nations do, is that Australian historians in their fascination with the development of political, economic and social institutions have left the churches' history on one side because there seemed to be more urgent tasks. In other cases, there was a rejection of family religious loyalties as in Russel Ward, or their re-interpretation as in Manning Clark. Clark may not agree with the ethos of evangelical protestantism, but his readers are left in no doubt about the impact of personal and cultural sin in Australian Christianity, or the importance of the issues with which Australian Christians dealt with less than adequately.

O'Farrell's comments on the derivative nature of our Christianity rightly reject the general view that religion has been neither vital, nor irrelevant. "An uneasy tension exists between some sort of feeling of spiritual need and the repulsion of the elements of foreignness or falsity in what is offered to satisfy it." He blames the secular school system for the non-philosophical tenor of Australian society and for the remarkable ignorance of religion which fortified and deepened the convict tradition that devotees of religion were "traitors to genuine national traditions of behaviour".

He does not mention the secular tradition of the universities and their corporate lack of interest in the teaching of philosophy, religion and ethics for all graduates. Nor does he do justice to the remarkable way in which the Australian churches did so much to remove popular ignorance of religion among classes from Britain whose religious poverty was immense. If they did not succeed, neither did the high-culture churches of Europe.

> The relationship between the secular and religious elements and tendencies in Australian culture and society continues to be uncertain, complex, ambivalent. Or is it merely that the question of that relationship, being unpopular and foreign among the secularized intelligentsia, has remained neglected, unstudied? All the indicators are that religion—or the lack of it—can tell a great deal about the history and nature of Australian culture.[13]

Australian Accents

Even more interesting in the persistence of religion is the way in which some of the churches have built up their own networks for theological education, which compare very favourably with those available in Britain. There are a significant number of scholars who have given the Australian churches a theological depth that has not existed before.[14] The educational resources published by the Joint Board of Christian Education and Collins Dove match anything overseas. The growth of overseas aid agencies suggests that there are still elements of compassion and generosity that can be tapped outside the churches. Indeed, the contribution of Australian Christians to the work of churches and humanitarian development overseas in personnel and resources may be considerably higher proportionally than in the United States. The Anglican Prayer Book, the Australian Hymn Book and its superb *Companion* by Wesley Milgate, Bruce Prewer's *Australian Psalms*, together with the music and hymnody of Chris Willcock, are signs of religious vitality, despite some evidence of institutional decline.

There are a surprising number of religious books now published in Australia, plus a variety of magazines and periodicals. The National Research Centre set up by Roman Catholics and the Zadok Centre in Canberra represent a major change in direction for pragmatic Christians. They, like Australian Frontier, have offered forums for reflection on the Australian scene, for it is becoming increasingly evident that more is required for the future of our past than the building of churches and the provision of clergy. The networks provided by Scaffolding in Sydney and the too little noted work of ITIM have given Australians leadership in urban mission.[15] The ABC Religious Affairs Unit has managed an amazingly high quality and variety of output despite its slender resources. Even if we lack electronic churches and tele-evangelists, some may think that a deliverance, while still deploring the culpable failure of the commercial TV channels to deal with religious and cultural matters with even a fraction of the depth the independent companies have provided in Britain.[16] There are modest signs of Christian presence in literature, and the exploration of broadly religious themes in the poetry of J. S. Nielson, James McAuley and Les Murray.[17] Novelists like Thomas Keneally have explored the idiosyncrasies, ironies and temptations of religion. Such themes are not absent from Patrick White and Christina Stead. There have not yet been great spiritual guides, but Mary McKillop's writings to her sisters are an astonishingly rich source of spirituality, which Australians must get to know better. Ukrainian church music has yet to influence the other major churches, but our provincialism is slowly eroding as the universal Christian heritage becomes more accessible to all Australian Christians.

There is still one major cultural and spiritual blind spot which impoverishes Australian Christianity—neglect of and contempt for Aboriginal religion in its primal and Christian forms. There are only faint signs of parallels to the adaptation and incorporation of the religions of the Celts and Anglo-Saxons into British Christianity, which released such spiritual and cultural energies in our ancestors. Yet, in the last two decades, there are some hopeful signs that learning from Aboriginal religion may have begun.

That has been underlined in three different ways. Firstly, the John Paul II's address to the great gathering of Aboriginal people at Alice Springs in 1986 is full of significant suggestions for partnership and interaction. Secondly, there are now for the first time an articulate group of Aboriginal leaders who have been educated in the European theological pattern, but who can speak with pride and authority about their own spiritual heritage and the presence of the Father in their own cultures. The language they use may be unfamiliar. Protestants have had great difficulty in dealing with the reality of a mythology which does not have the kinds of historical roots with which they are familiar. Thirdly, the formation of The Uniting Aboriginal and Islander Christian Congress in 1985 has provided a base for action throughout Australia, within and beyond the Uniting Church.

The writings of the Rev. Djiniyini Gondarra, a former Moderator of the Northern Synod of the Uniting Church and staff member at Nungalinya College, Darwin, are a vivid reminder that "thinking black" offers different perspectives on the Christian tradition at a number of points. He has also been one of the leaders in a religious revival on Elcho Island, which has spread into the Northern Territory and into both West Australia and Queensland. It has a strong link with charismatic styles and has had remarkable success in transforming not only individuals, but whole communities. Unmistakably aboriginal, it is an adaptation on aboriginal terms of basic themes in the Christian heritage.[18]

Aboriginals have not simply been victims of white missionary work. Many of the records show how skilfully tribal communities kept alive crucial elements of their custom, while at the same time using the missionaries for their own agenda. One of the most interesting studies of this process, widely recognised in other countries is the study by Peter Willis of the conversion of a Miriwung group to Catholicism, near Kununurra in 1969. He underlines the creativity of the Aboriginal adaptation and the ways in which they expected reciprocal learning from the priest.[19]

The period since 1945 has seen many changes from the paternalism that characterised both Church and Government policy after 1945. The war brought many changes, not least, opportunity to earn wages hitherto undreamt of. Trade unions, politicians and missionaries slowly began to realise a new era had dawned. Some missionaries continued the old paternalism until the 1970s, despite the changes in government policy before and after the Referendum in 1967, which conferred the franchise on Aboriginal people and even led to the election of Senator Neville Bonner from Queensland. All the major churches involved with missions to traditional people began by the 'seventies to move towards devolution of responsibility and the education of leaders.[20]

The continued consequences of that paternalism can be seen in the Aboriginal communities which stood in the way of mining development. Though some of the missionaries gained what they thought was some protection from the incursions of mining, they were outmanouvered by skilled negotiators who gained access to enormous mineral resources. The community at Mapoon in Queensland was moved with no compensation in 1963, for by law, aboriginal people had no property rights. They simply had to leave houses and possessions behind, with no compensation.

Similar events occurred at Weipa and Aurukun. The latter in particular, was a baptism of fire for the newly-formed Uniting Church, which vainly attempted to secure a modicum of consultation and justice for the people which the Presbyterian Church had served since the beginning of the century. The Queensland government exploited the political vacuum between the dismissal of Mr. Whitlam in 1975 and the consequent election to push through an act permitting mining at Aurukun. They were resisted by leaders of the Queensland Synod of the Uniting Church led by Professor R. Busch and supported by Dr. John Brown of the Commission on Mission in Sydney. They were outmanouvered by Mr. Bjelke-Petersen and his ministers and advisers, despite an attempt by the Uniting Church to invoke the constitutional powers of the Federal government. Mr. Fraser was not prepared to face a confrontation and the result was a defeat.[21] To this day the Queensland government had steadfastly refused to give any general security of title to Aboriginal and Islander people, except in small parcels which have no mineral significance. And the Aurukun Shire Council set up in 1978, still has not had its by-laws ratified.

Nor has the Hawke government honoured its electoral commitment to establish uniform land rights federally. Important reports like those by Mr. Justice Woodward in 1974 have gone some way to developing a base for legislation based on corporate title, but at the present there appears to be little political will for this most fundamental acts of social justice.[22] Graziers and miners alike see a threat to their interests and profits. The proposal, worked out by Father Frank Brennan, S.J. with the support of all the major churches, for a Parliamentary Declaration as the first act in the new parliament buildings opened in 1988, fell foul of those interests and fears. That showed yet again what a major task the churches face if they wish to be committed to partnership with Aboriginal Christians and seek appropriate communal forms of repentance for dispossession in the name of development.

As they faced intractable issues of this kind, a number of leaders of Australian churches developed a new style of witness and persuasion. Instead of relying on the informal processes of consultation, or official pronouncements, they have researched particular issues—often ecumenically. By such focus on particular issues, governments have often been moved to take action, whereas they could safely ignore homiletic exhortations.[23] The work of the Australian Inland Mission in the development of the new mining towns of the North West, is one example of that. The dignified and factual plea for the poor by Archbishop Loane against the bluster of the Prime Minister, Mr. McMahon, led to the Henderson Enquiry on Poverty and far reaching recommendations on social policy. Dealing with issues which go deep into the nation's life like poverty and peace, has caused deep tensions within the churches, because of the strength of the old liberal tradition and anxiety that the spiritual and temporal are being confused, and the primacy of personal transformation ignored.[24]

Conclusion

Australian Christians worked for a society which recognised the equality of all religions before the law, and encouraged the liberty of conscience. Protestants believed this was the most secure foundation for a Christian society. They were opposed to the alternative—a nation with an established Church. Catholics were equally determined to be equal partners in nation-building, but they were not to gain full equality until the 1960s, when educational and employment barriers largely disappeared.

The novelty of Australian choices stands out when Australian Church history is compared with that of church parent bodies in Britain and Ireland, or with the history of the other British colonies of settlement. Initial establishment of the Church of England as a prison chaplaincy was not a promising beginning. That exclusive position was soon challenged and the Bourke Church Acts were a remarkable experiment in partnership between Church and State, removing disabilities from other Churches long before similar reforms in Britain. The state aid given in most colonies was indispensable to the major churches. Before the abolition of aid, they met a major expansion of population in the 19th century, without having wholly to rely on their own resources.

Colonial governments welcomed the civilising influence of the Churches. Even after state aid to religion and education was abolished, there was broad agreement that the major moral emphases of Christianity were essential for the well-being of the colonies. Disagreement occurred over the boundaries of that common morality, and how best to ensure acceptance of that ethic. The Churches disagreed among themselves on both issues. So it was not surprising that they did not wholly persuade the Australian colonists. Yet they managed a degree of success which made British visitors feel that the authority of the Churches here compared very favourably with the influence of the home Churches.

This mission to former convicts and free settlers relied on the building of Churches and the provision of clergy and religious. Buildings were often primitive and makeshift, but the networks of commitment established were strong and enduring. Settlers learned to be self-supporting financially in religious affairs. A local ministry had emerged by the end of the 19th century and the Australian Churches were self-governing, despite their close spiritual ties with parent bodies. There was a much greater degree of lay participation in church government here than in parent churches. Nineteenth century religious demography has been slow to change. Roman Catholics have only just edged Anglicans out of first place in census statistics.

This is largely as the result of migration, which has modified the original religious spectrum, especially since 1945. Australia also now has members of all the great Christian families, making Christianity far more catholic than it had been and potentially capable of enriching and inspiring national life. Yet the Churches have still to win their way, rather than rely on historic status. Migration always loosens religious commitment. So ancient rivalries and enmities have diminished, even disappeared, as migrants lived and worked alongside hither to unknown or feared groups which had been far removed by geography and culture.

That aspect of religious equality has been one of the most important achievements of the last two centuries, even if it was not always the choice of Church leaders concerned to maintain historic identity. Practical co-operation locally and official co-operation regionally has been far ahead of Britain and Europe's more limited progress in that direction. There have been no religious wars, despite the presence of flammable materials among migrants. Since the 1960s, the astonishing development of ecumenism has broken down many emotional and institutional walls. In part Australian in origin, in part a response to dramatic changes in Rome, Constantinople, Geneva and Canterbury, the energies released have great potential for enhancing national unity.

Such changes raise sharply issues of Christian identity. When that is no longer defined by rivalry, suspicion and enmity, fresh attention must be paid to the common foundations of Christian faith. Australian Christians have hitherto not been notable for theological or spiritual creativity. They have preferred to adapt insights from Europe and America. Given the greater religious pluralism and multiculturalism of contemporary Australia, Christians will need to rediscover their heritage and interpret it more contextually if the present generation is to have the same missionary impact as did our 19th century forbears. They played an important part in the transformation of a corrupt, ignorant and irresponsible society. Current challenges are different, but there are similar elements of corruption and irresponsibility about our physical and spiritual environment which demand far more than political and economic answers.

One of the most crucial challenges ahead for the Churches is learning from Aboriginal people how to be partners in the wide red land. The racism of two centuries is still alive and well, but for the first time there are the beginnings of a strong Aboriginal Christian voice which few white Christians have yet heard. Integrating a theology of land with wealth creation offers a fascinating challenge, if it is to be linked with social justice and the creation of a new kind of community that includes equal opportunity for all Australians to discover their divine image.

Achieving that in a deliberately secular nation is not a unique challenge in a world context. Nevertheless, Australian Christians have to appreciate both the positive and negative features of that secularity. Their experience has something to offer to other Churches working with similar issues. A better understanding of the rich variety of the resources on which they can draw both locally and ecumenically could ensure an exciting future for Australia's Christian past. Australia has had its fair share of godlessness, inherited from Britain and Europe. Yet the successes and persistence of Christianity have been surprising, given such unpromising beginnings. There is much evidence to suggest that such a combination of weakness and strength will continue to bewilder historians and puzzle Christians during our third century in this continent.

Notes

Chapter One: From Prison to Colony

1. A. Grocott, *Convicts, Clergymen and Churches*, Sydney, 1980; R. Hughes, *The fatal shore*, London, 1987.

2. J. Woolmington, *Religion in early Australia*, Sydney, 1977, pp. 143–44.

3. N.K. Macintosh, *Richard Johnson*, Sydney, 1978; I.H. Murray, *Australian Christian life from 1788*, Edinburgh, 1988, pp. 3 ff.; P. & D. O'Farrell, *Documents in Australian Catholic history*, 2 vols, London, 1969, 1.7 for the Roman Catholic offer.

4. A.T. Yarwood, *Samuel Marsden*, Melbourne,1977; S. Judd and K. Cable, *Sydney Anglicans*, Sydney, 1987, pp. 4 ff. I am deeply indebted to their study at many points.

5. O'Farrell, *Documents*, 1.73–74; P. O'Farrell, *The Catholic Church and community*, Sydney, 1985, cap 1. This is an indispensable work, but there are additional insights in E. Campion, *Australian Catholics*, Melbourne, 1987. See also J. O'Riordan, *Irish Catholic tradition and practice*, Dublin, 1980.

6. M. Nicholls, (ed) *The diary of the Rev. Robert Knopwood*, Hobart, 1977.

7. *Parliamentary Debates*, Queensland, 1985, p 2396. I owe this reference to Father F.J. Brennan S.J.T. Mayne, *Aborigines and the issues*, Sydney, 1986 is an indispensable bibliography. J. Woolmington, *Aborigines in colonial society*, Sydney, 1973 has a useful collection of documents. M. Wilson, *Ministry among aboriginal people*, Melbourne 1988, has a useful survey of Roman Catholic missions. J. Harris, *Christianity in Aboriginal Australia*, Canberra, 1987—deals with the whole scene.

8. D.J. Mulvaney & J.P. White, *Australians. To 1788*, Sydney, 1987, pp. 216–17, 350–51; W.H. Stanner, *Aboriginal religion*, Sydney, 1963; R. & C. Berndt, *Australian Aboriginal religion*, Leiden, 1974; T. Swain, *Interpreting Aboriginal religion*, Adelaide, 1985.

9. I. Bradley, *The Call to Seriousness*, London, 1976.

10. J. Bossy, *Christianity in the West*, Oxford, 1985 gives an account of the process.

11. A. C. Nelson, *History of the effective establishment of Congregationalism*, Hobart, 1930.

12. D.W.A. Baker, *Days of wrath*, Melbourne, 1985.

13. M. Hoban, *Caroline Chisholm*, Melbourne, 1984; R. Teale, *Colonial Eve*, Melbourne, 1978, pp. 57 ff.

14. G.P. Shaw, *Patriarch and patriot*, Melbourne, 1978; Judd and Cable, *op. cit.*, pp. 19 ff.

15. O'Farrell, *Catholic Church*, p. 19.

16. F. O'Donoghue, *Bishop of Botany Bay*, Sydney, 1982.

17. C.T. Stannage, (ed.) *New history of Western Australia*, Perth, 1981, pp. 575–598; J. Tonkin, *Religion and society in Western Australia*, Perth 1987; C. Jenkins, *A History of Methodism in Western Australia*, Perth, 1930; W. McNair & H. Rumley, *Pioneer Aboriginal mission*, Perth, 1981.

18. C.C. Dugan, *A century of Tasmanian Methodism*, Hobart, 1920, pp. 11–12, 107–109.

19. W.H. Fysh, *Henry Reed*, Hobart, 1975.

Chapter Two: Christianisation of Australia

1. Judd & Cable, *op. cit.*, pp. 26 ff. for the impact of the Church Acts.

2. J.H. Burleigh, *Church history of Scotland*, Oxford, 1960 pp. 334ff. for the Disruption; K.R. Campbell, "Presbyterian conflicts in New South Wales", *Journal of Religious History*, (*JRH*) 5.3. (1969) pp. 223 ff; Hamilton's journals are held in the National Library Canberra, MS 2117.

3. T.Q. Stow, *Congregationalism*, Sydney, 1855, pp. 10, 13; G.L. Lockley, *The foundation and development and influence of Congregationalism*, Ph.D.

thesis, University of Queensland, 1968, is invaluable. He has kindly granted permission to use material from his thesis.

4. D. Hilliard & A. Hunt, "Religions" in *Flinders History of South Australia*, Adelaide, 1987, pp. 194 ff. is a model of the kind of overview needed for each state and territory. B. Dickey, *Holy Trinity*, Adelaide, 1988, breaks new ground in writing parish history. D. Schubert, *Kavel's people*, Adelaide, 1985, is a fine collection of documents on Lutheran beginnings.

5. D. Harris *et al.* (eds) *The shape of belief*, Sydney, 1987, pp. 229 ff. A more complete historical survey of religious statistics is found in W. Vamplew, *Australians. Historical statistics*, Sydney, 1987. M.R. McGinley and T. Kelly, *The Church's mission in Australia*, Melbourne, 1988, pp. 2–3 point out that the Australian Capital Territory now has the highest percentage of Roman Catholics—30%.

6. W.C. Pritchard, *Sydney Linton*, Melbourne, 1896 p. 22; B. Hodge, *Remembered with pride*, Sydney, 1988, p. 60.

7. K. Rayner, *History of the Church of England in Queensland*, Ph.D. thesis, University of Queensland, 1962, p. 397. Dr. Janet Scarfe notes interest in 'common Christianity' in South Australia in her *Bridge of steel as fine as hair*, M.A. Thesis, University of Adelaide, 1976. S. Piggin, *Faith of Steel*, Wollongong, 1984, for demoninational vitality in The Illawarra.

8. Battye Library MN 257 Trinity 2992A/s contains the relevant Trinity Church records.

9. K.H. Addison, *History of Lutwyche parish*, p. p. 1951, pp. 9–10.

10. M. Petras, (ed.) *Australian Baptists*, Sydney, 1988, p. 10 for the Gibsons. Principal Manley gave me this reference.

11. J.T.R. Border, *The founding of the see of Goulburn*, Canberra, 1956.

12. J. Colwell, *Illustrated history of Methodism*, Sydney, 1904, pp. 377 ff. R. Sutherland, *History of the Presbyterian Church of Victoria*, London, 1877, pp. 76 ff. for these beginnings.

13. N. Batt & M. Roe, "Conflict within the Church of England in Tasmania", *JRH* 4.1 (1967) pp. 39 ff; D. Hilliard, *Godliness and good order*, Adelaide, 1986, pp. 20–21.

14. J.T.R. Border, *Church and state in Australia*, London, 1962; A. De. Q. Robin, *Charles Perry*, Perth 1967; Judd and Cable, *op. cit.*, 52 ff.

15. J. Hussey, *Henry Backhaus*, Bendigo, 1982.

16. G.M. Griffin & D. Tobin, *In the midst of life*, Melbourne, 1982, pp. 29 ff; R. Mole, *Cornerstones*, Adelaide, 1980, pp. 14–15.

17. G.R. Quaife, "Money and men", *JRH* 5.1. (1968) pp. 45 ff. on Victorian expansion. The Battye Library has Parry's letters. MN 73/996A. For South Australia see A.D. Hunt. *This side of heaven*, Adelaide, 1985, pp. 117 ff.

18. R.B. Walker, "The growth and typology of the Wesleyan Methodist Church in New South Wales", *JRH*, 6.4. (1971) pp. 331 ff; R. Howe, "Social composition of the Wesleyan Church in Victoria during the nineteenth century", *JRH* 4:3 (1967) pp. 206–17; J.C. Symons, *Life of Rev. Daniel James Draper*, London, 1870.

19. D. Hilliard, *Popular revivalism*, Adelaide, 1982.

20. W.J. Lawton, *The better time to be*, University of NSW, Sydney, 1990. R. Teale, *Colonial Eve*, pp. 184–85 for women's part in the Grubb mission.

21. A.G. Austin, (ed.) *Select documents in Australian education*, Melbourne, 1963; idem, *Australian education*, Melbourne, 1961.

22. O'Farrell, *Catholic Church*, pp. 138 ff.; N. Turner, *Sinews of sectarian warfare*, Canberra, 1972; J.S. Gregory, *Church and state*, Melbourne, 1973; R. Fogarty, *Catholic education in Australia*, 2 vols, Melbourne, 1959; G. Haines, *Lay Catholics and the education question*, Sydney, 1976.

23. W.W. Phillips, *Defending "A Christian country"*, Brisbane, 1981; J.D. Bollen, *Protestantism and social reform in New South Wales*, Melbourne, 1972.

24. K. Dunstan, *Wowsers*, Melbourne, 1968; S. Willis, (ed) *Faith and fetes*, Melbourne, 1977, pp. 43 ff. for the Women's Christian Temperance Union in Victoria.

25. H.R. Jackson, *Churches and people in Australia and New Zealand*, Wellington, 1987, pp. 125 ff.

26. J.W.S. Tomlin, *The story of the Bush Brotherhoods*, London, 1949.

27. Phillips, *op. cit.*, pp. 113 ff.; C. Badger, *The Revd Charles Strong and the Australian Church*, Melbourne, 1971.

28. W.O. Lilley, *Reminiscences*, Brisbane, 1913, p. 91; C.H. Spence, *An autobiography*, Adelaide, 1910; M.F. Sugden, *Edward. H. Sugden*, Melbourne, 1941; Hunt *op. cit.*, pp. 261–2.

29. D. Wright, *Mantle of Christ*, Brisbane, 1984; W. Palamountain, *A.R. Edgar*, Melbourne, 1933; G. Davison, (ed). *Outcasts of Melbourne*, Melbourne, 1985; W.G. Spence, *Australia's Awakening*, Sydney, 1909.

30. R.G. Ely, *Unto God and Caesar*, Melbourne, 1976.

31. J. Harris, *Christianity in Aboriginal Australia*, Canberra, 1987; E. Leske, *Herrmansburg*, Adelaide, 1977; D. Harris, *op. cit.*, pp. 132, 159; CCJP, *Aboriginal Land rights*, Sydney, 1985.

32. J.B. Gribble, *Dark deeds in a sunny land*, Perth, 1905; *West Australian*, 24th August, 1886. I owe this reference to Bob Tonkinson's introduction to the 1987 re-issue of Gribble.

33. A. DeQ. Robin, "Theology and theological training", *Royal Australian Historical Society Journal*, 54 (1968) pp. 356 ff. D. Chambers, *Theological teaching and thought in the Theological Hall of the Presbyterian Church of Victoria*, Melbourne, 1967; M. Loane, *Centenary history of Moore College*, Sydney, 1955; K. Livingston, *The emergence of an Australian Catholic priesthood*, Sydney, 1977.

Chapter Three: Fulfilment of the Kingdom

1. H.F. Tucker, (ed.) *The Church in the Commonwealth*, Melbourne,1901, p.120

2. *West Australian*, 19 October, 1899.

3. O'Farrell, *Catholic Church*, pp. 350–52.

4. Willis, *op. cit.*, pp. 94 ff. on Holmes; K. Cole, *Robert Harkness*, Bendigo, 1988.

5. R. Broome, *Treasure in earthen vessels*, Brisbane, 1980, pp. 126 ff.

6. B. Judd, *He that doeth*, London, 1951.

7. Broome, *op. cit.*, pp. 74 ff.; F. Engel, *Australian Christians in conflict and unity*, Melbourne, 1984; C. Uidam, "Why the church union movement failed in Australia, 1901–25", *JRH*, 13.4 (1984–5) pp. 393 ff.

8. National Library, Ferguson MS NL 3408. I am grateful for permission to use this material.

9. *Parliamentary Debates*, Victoria, vol. 125, p. 1964.

10. Oxley Library MSS OM 71–51 *Garland Letters;* OM 66–5 *Bible in State Schools League.*

11. M. McKenzie, *Mission to Arnhem Land,* Adelaide, 1976; E. Perez, *Kalumburu,* Kalumburu, 1977; F. X. Gsell, *The Bishop with 150 wives,* Sydney, 1956; K. Cole, *From Mission to church,* Bendigo, 1985.

12. G. Higgins, *James Noble,* Sydney, 1981; M.T. Clark, *Pastor Doug,* Melbourne, 1965.

13. W.A. Long, *Harry Foster,* p. p. 1946; *Bobbie Peters,* Alice Springs, n. d.

14. K. Cole, *History of the Church Missionary Society,* Sydney, 1971, p. 179; A. Dyer, *Unarmed Combat,* Sydney (1934?)

15. M. Morgan, *A drop in a bucket,* Melbourne, 1986; M. Durack, *The rock and the sand,* London, 1969; E.A. Worms, *Australian Aboriginal religions,* Sydney, 1986.

16. F. O'Grady, *Francis of Central Australia,* Sydney, 1977.

17. W.S. McPheat, *John Flynn,* London, 1963; Plowman's correspondence is held in the National Library, Canberra, MS/NL 1941.

18. M. McKernan, *Australian churches at war,* Sydney, 1980; P. Hancox, *Cavalry or Calvary,* Brisbane, 1984 for a conscientious objector's story.

19. R. Trumble, *Kenneth Thorne Henderson,* Melbourne, 1988; R.G. MacIntyre, *The other side of death,* London, 1920.

20. T.P. Boland, *James Duhig,* Brisbane, 1986; O'Farrell, *Catholic Church,* pp. 298 ff.; M. Hogan, *The sectarian strand,* Melbourne, 1987.

21. Hilliard, *Godliness and good order,* pp. 87–91; Judd and Cable, *op. cit.,* pp. 191 ff.

22. D.A. Pear, *Two Anglican responses to the Depression and Second World War,* M.Th. thesis, Melbourne College of Divinity, 1985; J. Handfield, *Friends and Brothers,* Melbourne, 1980.

23. G. Henderson, *Mr. Santamaria and the bishops,* Sydney, 1982; B.A. Santamaria, *Against the tide,* Melbourne, 1981.

24. D. McNeill, (ed.) *The MacKays of Drummartin and Sunshine,* Melbourne, 1984; R.V. Ord, *R.J. Gilbertson Pty.,* Melbourne, 1978.

25. D. Parker, *Fundamentalism and conservative Protestantism in Australia, 1920–80*, Ph. D. thesis, University of Queensland, 1982; B. Chant, *Heart of fire*, Adelaide, 1984.

26. A. Dougan, *A backward glance at the Angus affair*, Sydney, 1971; S. Emilsen, *Samuel Angus and the Presbyterian Church*, Ph. D. thesis, University of Sydney, 1985; D. Garnsey, *Arthur Garnsey*, Sydney, 1984; S. Emilsen, *A whiff of heresy*, Sydney, 1990.

27. O'Farrell, *Catholic Church*, pp. 388 ff; Hunt, *op. cit.*, 303 ff. J. Raftery, *Till every foe is vanquished*, Ph.D. thesis, Flinders University, 1988, discusses church attitudes in South Australia between 1919-39. D.E. Hansen, *The churches and society in New South Wales*, 1919-39 Ph.D thesis, Macquarie University, 1978. B. Condon has edited Anglican and Methodist statements in South Australia.

Chapter Four: Towards a Catholic Australia

1. B. Mansfield, "The churches' voice", in A. Dutney, (ed) *From here to where*, Melbourne, 1988.

2. The earlier background is discussed in J. Mansfield, "The Social Gospel in the Church of England in New South Wales, in the 1930s", *JRH*, 13.4. (1984–85) pp. 411 ff.

3. M. Loane, *Archbishop Mowll*, London, 1960.

4. T.C. Hammond, (ed) *The Bathurst Ritual case*, Sydney [1949?]; R. Teale, "The Red Book Case", JRH, 12.1, (1982–83) pp. 74 ff.

5. J. Davis, *Continuity and change*, Th.D thesis, Melbourne College of Divinity, 1987, is a comprehensive account of the 1962 Constitution.

6. C. Uidam, *Union and renewal*, Sydney; 1970; R.J. Lucy, *Presbyterian politics*, Ph.D thesis, University of NSW, 1976.

7. J.D. McCaughey, "Church union in Australia", *Ecumenical Review*, 17 (1965) pp. 38 ff.; "Confessions of faith in union negotiations", *Midstream*, 6.3 (1967).

8. D. Hynd, Australian *Christianity in outline*, Sydney, 1984, pp. 4 ff., for some recent statistics and their possible meaning; Harris, *op. cit.*, pp. 70 ff.

9. W.H. Paech, *Twelve decades of grace*, Adelaide, 1974.

10. D. Harris, *op. cit.*, pp. 95 ff.; H. Simmons, *Orthodoxy in Australia*, Brookline, 1986; A.W. Ata (ed) *Religion and ethnic identity*, Melbourne, 1988, pp. 152 ff.

11. M. Rinvolucri, *Anatomy of a church*, London, 1955, gives a helpful description of the Orthodox Church in Greece.

12. Hunt, *op. cit.*, pp. 370 ff. for the impact of the Wells Organisation and Stewardship. Judd and Cable, *op. cit.* pp. 267 ff. have an excellent discussion of the major financial reorganisation of Sydney's Anglican diocese under Archbishop Gough.

13. A. Amos, *The Rev. Graeme Bucknall in ministry*, Melbourne, 1985; C. Williams, *Where in the world?*, New York, 1963; *Faith in a secular age*, London, 1966.

14. Battye Library MSS MN 112 *Archbishop Moline*.

15. McGinley and Kelly, *op. cit.*, pp. 4–8 for migrant origins. F. Lewins, *The myth of the universal church*, Canberra, 1978. A. Pitarello, *Soup without salt*, Sydney, 1980. Harris, *op. cit.*, pp. 89 ff.

16. P. Merchant, *History, evolution, function and contribution of the Catholic Immigration Office in Melbourne*, 1949–85, Melbourne, 1985.

17. M. Saunders & R. Summy, *The Australian Peace Movement*, Canberra, 1986; M. Hartley, *The truth shall prevail*, Melbourne, 1982.

18. B.A. Santamaria, "The movement" in H. Mayer (ed.) *Catholics in a free society*, Melbourne, 1961, pp. 54 ff.; N. Brennan, *The politics of Catholics*, Melbourne, 1972, gives a hostile account of the Movement.

19. R.G. Ely, "The forgotten nationalism. Australian Protestantism in the Second World War," *Journal of Australian Studies*, No. 20, 1987. See also, G.C. Bolton, *Dick Boyer*, Canberra, 1967.

20. Hunt, *op. cit.*, pp. 394 ff.; H.P. Phillips, *Memories and reflections*, Melbourne, 1974, pp. 51–55.

21. O'Farrell, *Catholic Church*, p.413.

22. J.A. Connellan, *Christian unity in God's way*, Melbourne, p.4.

23. M. Hogan, *The Catholic campaign for State Aid*, Sydney, 1978; J. Woodward, "The turmoil of State Aid', *Brisbane Catholic Historical Society*, I (1988) pp. 52–62.

24. D.F. Cave, *Percy Jones*, Melbourne, 1988, pp. 89 ff.

25. W.J. Lawton, *That woman Jezebel,—Moore College after twenty-five years,* Sydney, 1981.

26. S.B. Babbage & I. Siggins, *Light beneath the Southern Cross,* Melbourne, 1960; A. Nichols and W. Olson, *Crusading down under,* Minneapolis, 1970; Judd and Cable, *op. cit.,* pp. 256 ff.; Hunt, *op. cit.,* pp. 367 ff. R. Mathias, *Mission to the nation,* Melbourne, 1986; H. Whitney, *Tell Australia,* Brisbane, 1958; H. Henderson, *Reach for the world,* Nashville, 1981.

Chapter Five: Future of our Past

1. I. Gillman, (ed) *Many faiths, one nation,* Melbourne, 1988; R. Humphreys & R. Ward, *Religious bodies in Australia,* Melbourne, 1988; H. Mol, *The faith of Australians* , Sydney, 1985. M. Mason and G. Fitzpatrick (eds.), *Religion in Australian life,* Sydney, 1982.

2. P.H. Cock, *Alternative Australia,* Melbourne, 1979; N. Preston, *Christian communities in Australia* , Melbourne, 1982; M. Britt, *In search of new wineskins,* Melbourne, 1988 p. 31.

3. Britt, *ibid.,* p.26; G. Moon, "Household Church groups in Canberra," *Interchange,* 3.2 (1971) pp. 101–16; R. Banks, *The home church,* Sydney, 1986; J. Smith, *On the side of the Angels,* London, 1987; D. Prince, *Tuned into change,* Sydney, 1979.

4. Chant, *op. cit.,* pp. 219 ff.; R. Doyle, *Signs and wonders and Evangelicals,* Sydney, 1987.

5. R.B. Flowers, *Religion in strange times,* Macon, 1984; A. Hastings, *History of English Christianity,* London, 1986, both give helpful surveys of this period.

6. E. Campion, *Rockchoppers,* Melbourne, 1982; R.J. Selleck, *Crudden,* Melbourne, 1970; M. Parer and T. Peterson, *Prophets and losses in the priesthood,* Sydney, 1971; N. Blaikie, *The plight of the Australian clergy,* Brisbane, 1979.

7. K. Giles, *Created woman,* Canberra, 1987; S. Willis, *Adventure into feminism,* Canberra, 1983; D. Wetherell (ed), *Women priests in Australia,* Melbourne, 1987; M. Tulip, *Women in a man's church,* Sydney, 1983; M.L. Porter, *Women in the church,* Melbourne, 1989.

8. Until there is a study of the Australian Protestants, J. Dillenberger & C. Welch, *Protestantism,* London, 1988, provides an excellent survey. J.A. Conellan, *Unity—the work of God,* Melbourne, 1947, p. 15 suggested

that "Protestantism continues to disintegrate and decompose until there is no particle of the original faith that is not denied." S. Piggin, "Bicentennial History of Australian Evangelicalism," *Lucas* No. 4, September 1988.

9. M. Hogan, "Australian secularists", *Journal for the Scientific Study of Religion*, 18 (1979) pp. 390 ff.; G.D. Bouma & B. Dixon, *The religious factor in Australian life*, Melbourne, 1986, pp. 166–67; N. Salan, "The secularisation of Australian society," *Trinity Occasional papers*, 7.1 (1988) pp. 37–46; R.D. Linder, "Civil religion in America and Australia", *Lucas* No.3, 1988; R. Ireland, *Challenge of Secularisation*, Melbourne, 1988.

10. D. Wright, *Mantle of Christ*, p. 215.

11. R. Conway, *The end of stupor*, Melbourne, 1984; *Conway's way*, Melbourne, 1988.

12. Mitchell MSS Margaret McIntyre 1158/1–5; D. McNeill *op cit.* pp. 18,21 for the religious practice of the McKay family; B. Lewis, *Sunday at Kooyong Road*, Melbourne, 1976.

13. P. O'Farrell, "The cultural ambivalence of Australian religion", in *Studies in Australian cultural history*, Canberra, 1982, pp. 6,7,8.

14. R. Banks, "Fifty years of Theology," *Colloquium*, 11 (1978) pp. 7–16; E.F. Osborn, "Tendencies in Australian Theology" *Colloquium* 12 (1979) pp. 2–16; V. Hayes (ed) *Towards theology in an Australian Context*, Adelaide, 1979.

15. L. Styles, *Direction signs to an achievable future*, Melbourne, 1982; F. Engel, *Australian Frontier*, Melbourne, 1988.

16. J. Munro, "Some recollections on television", *St Mark's Review*, 74 (1973) pp. 22–26; J. Peter, *Principles of religious broadcasting*, Sydney, 1963.

17. L. Murray, (ed) *Anthology of Australian religious poetry*, Melbourne, 1986; V. Brady, *Crucible of prophets*, Sydney, 1981; N. Brown, *Faith and culture*, Sydney, 1978, pp. 1–9.

18. D. Gondarra, "Father you gave us the dreaming" in Dutney, *op. cit.*; L. Lamilami, *Lamilami speaks*, Sydney, 1971.

19. P. Willis, *Riders in the chariot*, Melbourne, 1987. That theme is underlined by R. Bos in his 1988 Ph.D. thesis, University of Queensland, *Jesus and the dreaming*.

20. United Church of North Australia, *Free to decide*, 1974 reflected the move from paternalism. See E. Wells, *Reward and punishment in Arnhem Land*, Canberra, 1982.

21. J. Harrison, *Baptism of fire*, Melbourne, 1987, pp. 27 ff. for an account of the Aurukun affair.

22. F.J. Brennan, "What must now be said," in Dutney, *op. cit;* CCJP, *Aboriginal land rights*, Sydney, 1985; K. Baker, (ed) *The land rights debate*, Melbourne, 1985; E.D. Stockton, *This land, our mother*, Sydney, 1986; I. Yule (ed) *My mother the land*, Galiwinku, 1980. C. Jacobs, *Healing a divided nation*, Perth, 1986, offers a dissenting view. J. Harris, *One blood*, Sydney, 1990.

23. Examples of the new approach can be seen in the debate over economics in G. Brennan *et al*. *Chaining Australia*, Sydney, 1984.

24. M. Gilchrist, *New church or true church*, Melbourne, 1987; P. Collins, *Mixed blessings*, Melbourne, 1986; G. Pell, *Catholicism in Australia*, Melbourne, 1988.